Quebec Nationalism in Crisis traces two antagonistic trends in recent Quebec history, both of which have aided the modernization of French society. The one is the growth of nationalism which reached its high point with the election of René Lévesque in 1967. The other is the development of a type of individualism favouring economic pursuits and personal development at the expense of group solidarity.

Nationalism began to assert itself in the 1960s with the emergence of the welfare state. The newly created bureaucracy challenged its federal counterpart, which was essentially English-speaking. It replaced the Catholic clergy as the ruling elite, and it formed the core of a new political coalition which would eventually take over power with the support of intellectuals, the educated classes, professionals, students, and organized labour.

As a result of changes occurring in the 1950s, including rapid urbanization and industrialization, a countervailing force appeared. The Créditiste movement was the first to challenge the growing power of the bureaucrats.

By the time of the referendum in 1980, the two opposing ideologies were in open competition. The ruling nationalist coalition was eager to bring in the nation-state while those who had not benefited from the new nationalist vision were on the side of federalism. The latter group included businessmen, women, the poor or less educated, along with the very rich, and it was successful in defeating sovereignty-association. However, it was unable to put the provincial Liberals into power in 1981.

Clift argues that a victory for antinationalist and federalist forces would not have restored the equilibrium of the federal system. Its historical balance has been disrupted by the growing strength of the French economy in Quebec. This has given rise to unforeseen problems of leadership and coordination in such a geographically large country as Canada.

Coauthor with Sheila McLeod Arnopoulos of *The English Fact in Quebec*, the French edition of which won the Governor-General's Award for non-fiction, Dominique Clift is well known as a journalist who has written for the *Globe and Mail*, the *Toronto Star*, the *Montreal Star*, and Canadian Press.

By the same author
THE ENGLISH FACT IN QUEBEC
In collaboration with Sheila McLeod Arnopoulos
McGill-Queen's University Press 1980

Dominique Clift

QUEBEC NATIONALISM IN CRISIS

McGill-Queen's University Press
Kingston and Montreal

ISBN 0-7735-0381-1 (cloth)
ISBN 0-7735-0383-8 (paper)

Legal deposit 1st quarter 1982
Bibliothèque nationale du Québec

This work was originally published in French in 1981 by
Editions Libre Expression under the title *Le déclin du nationalisme
au Québec*. It has been translated by the author, who has added
the Epilogue and the Suggestions for Further Reading to the
English edition. The translation and its publication have been
assisted by grants from the Canada Council.

Cover photo: *La Presse*

Printed in Canada

CANADIAN CATALOGUING IN PUBLICATION DATA

Clift, Dominique.
    Quebec nationalism in crisis

Translation of: Le déclin du nationalisme au Québec.
Includes bibliographical references.
ISBN 0-7735-0381-1 (bound). — ISBN 0-7735-0383-8
(pbk.)

1. Nationalism — Quebec (Province) — History.
2. Quebec (Province) — History — Autonomy and
independence movements. 3. Quebec (Province) —
Politics and government — 20th century.* I. Title.
FC2925.9.N3C5413   971.4'04   C81-095092-8
F1053.2.C5413

Contents

Foreword

After the referendum of May 1980, while working for Canadian Press, I wrote a series of articles seeking to explain why a majority of Quebec voters had rejected sovereignty-association and supported federalism. Two distinct trends impressed me at the time. One was the way in which popular sentiment had veered towards individualism and turned its back on collective values identified with nationalism. The other was the perceptible weakening of the social control exercised by various intellectual elites. It was on these two basic themes that I later composed this book.

The articles, entitled *The Decline of Nationalism in Quebec*, provoked interesting reactions. Some nationalists told me that if I were right in my analysis it meant the end of the French Fact and of social-democracy in Quebec. This was not a point of view I shared. Quebec's health is not necessarily linked to the strength of the nationalist movement. Indeed, at several periods of history, nationalism had proved to be a regressive and hindering influence. Moreover, nationalists are certainly not the only ones to be promoting a vigorous and flourishing French life in Quebec.

From the opposite camp, federalists expressed the idea that the decline of nationalism would usher in a new period of social progress. That too is open to doubt. There is no direct link between the two. Furthermore, such a view ignores the fact that the modernization of Quebec institutions over the last fifteen or twenty years depended on the ability of the nationalist movement to mobilize public sentiment to this end.

The series of articles, written in both English and French, appeared in many dailies outside Quebec. Among the various reactions reaching me, the most frequent one was relief. A very widespread view in English Canada was that once

Quebec had withdrawn some of its more extreme demands the former equilibrium of the federal system would be restored. Again, I do not think it will be so. The new situation could prove just as dangerous for Canadian institutions as was the rise of separatism. This is the problem discussed in the last chapter of this book.

I should also mention a commonly held opinion among liberals to the effect that nationalism is the principal obstacle to the acceptance of various ethnic groups into French society. It is worth stressing that pluralism and openness do not necessarily proceed from political creeds. Discrimination can have other causes than intolerance or cultural anxiety. It can also result from liberal indifference to the plight of different groups. It is inherent in bureaucratic organization where homogeneity and exclusiveness are enforced for the sake of efficiency and smooth operations.

What stands out at the present time is the lack of agreement on the role and the ideological content of nationalism. There is a strong tendency to consider it in absolute terms, positively or negatively according to circumstances and interest groups. It is in fact a cluster of ideas and feelings in constant flux.

This is what I have been exploring in the following essays on various aspects of nationalism in Quebec. I have attempted neither a historical outline nor a comprehensive description. My purpose has been to bring out its dominant traits, which people engaged in politics are often inclined to minimize or ignore completely.

The sense in which the word "nationalism" is used here is the one usually given to it in Quebec: the politicization of the sense of community. Or, if one prefers, the spilling over into the realm of politics of those feelings of solidarity, patriotism, and nationality possessed by any ethnic group. Similarly for liberalism, the meaning given to it is the one it has acquired in Quebec politics: first, in a general sense, the support of individual rights against the encroachments of statism and socialism; secondly, in a more specific sense, the refusal to subordinate individual and personal rights to national and collective goals, or even to religious goals as was the case before 1960.

Nationalism and Cultural Survival

Few political leaders in Quebec have left such a lively and contradictory image as Premier Maurice Duplessis. More than twenty years after his death in 1959, people can still be heard condemning certain political ideas or actions as "a return to the age of Duplessis." Others, given to nostalgia, deplore the absence in government of a strong hand capable of putting an end to the sterile confrontations paralysing Quebec and of setting it back on the right course.

The fascination he commands to this day cannot be explained solely by his personality, which dominated the province during a career spanning thirty years. Nor can one refer to his political thinking; although he had an intuitive grasp of crowd psychology and of the exercise of power, his ideas could hardly be described as subtle and did not transcend his times. Nor is the keen interest which he still arouses due to any similarity between the social and economic problems which plagued his times and those of the present generation. Quebec has changed so much in its makeup and organization that it would be risky to draw any parallel.

It is as if the image of Maurice Duplessis, like that of any colourful historical figure, were slowly being converted into folklore, a process which will ultimately anchor his memory in the popular mind. A very similar transformation into legend has kept alive the memory of Louis-Joseph Papineau, the Patriote leader of the 1837 Rebellion in Lower Canada. More than 150 years later he is still remembered as a symbol of mercurial intelligence and perceptiveness.

The traits of the legendary Duplessis are not yet fixed. Many negative characteristics predominate in the mental picture which most people have of him: authoritarianism, craftiness, and a readiness to make allowances for corruption among his close associates and his party. Yet he is also admired for restoring a strong sense of collective identity among a population which had always been disposed to act in an individualistic and selfish manner, almost to the point of anarchy. For the time being, he appeals primarily to those who hanker for authority and leadership.

The historical circumstances which propelled him to power, together with the rather unscrupulous and opportunistic use he made of nationalism, have largely been forgotten. His memory, however, does project a sense of involvement in a society currently experiencing great difficulty in maintaining a stable self-image in the face of constant and powerful external influences and pressures. Duplessis gave the appearance of a leader digging in his heels to forestall seemingly uncontrollable changes originating outside the province.

Present-day perception of Premier Duplessis may well involve the unconscious recognition of the anxiety felt during his day at the unwelcome prospect of social change and of the desperate efforts needed to ward it off. It is not necessarily that the present period shares the same fears or is adopting attitudes antagonistic to any transformation. But the unsettling effects of inflation over the last decade, among other things, have made people better aware of the tragic aspects of this recent historical period, one whose importance most French-speaking people tend to deny because of the feelings of powerlessness and inadequacy with which it is closely identified.

The most humiliating aspect of Duplessis's long reign, particularly the part following the Second World War, is its nationalism. It had a defensive and almost defeatist character which has become extremely distasteful to today's militant spirit. The group image derived from it is so negative as to impede understanding and sympathetic examination. It is difficult to take very seriously the dangers which this narrow-minded and isolationist ideology was supposed to ward off. While the doctrine itself has faded, renewed feelings of anxiety have contributed to a revival of interest in the former premier.

When Duplessis first took power, in 1936, he shared in the province's general desire for modernization and progress. His government launched several reform programs, notably the expansion of the elementary school network. The reckless spending of his administration, however, undermined the confidence of the public and of lending institutions. In 1939, with war seeming inevitable in Europe, he was caught on the middle ground between Liberals and nationalists. The former urged popular support for the war effort because they believed that military spending offered an unprecedented opportunity to expand the province's industrial base. The nationalists, on the other hand, pictured the war as just another British imperialist venture and campaigned for noninvolvement. Under these circumstances, the premier was unable to hang on to power. He was defeated in the elections he was forced to call late in 1939, as the banks refused to make credit available.

In 1944, when the Allies were assured of victory in Europe and Asia, Duplessis was returned to power. He had changed dramatically. His rather moderate nationalism had taken the form of an unshakeable opposition to any idea or trend which might threaten the historical trinity of *la foi, la langue, la race*—faith, language, and race—on which French cultural survival had long been said to depend. He became parsimonious in public spending and he refused to place his government at the mercy of financial institutions; public borrowing was held to a minimum and most capital expenditures were financed out of general tax revenues. He energetically promoted the airtight division of federal and provincial jurisdictions. Provincial autonomy became the rallying cry which helped keep the Union Nationale party, which he had founded, in power until 1960.

The type of nationalism identified with Premier Duplessis was meant to rally public opinion to the defence of traditional institutions. Prodded by the government, French society in postwar Quebec achieved a consensus which gave rise to the most smothering and tyrannical conformity it had ever known.

In spite of the confidence and optimism displayed in official circles, French Quebec felt so deeply threatened by the various pressures which would inevitably bring about fundamental social and economic changes that it could not even indulge in public discussion of them. It maintained a moratorium on such public debate which only a few intellectuals and trade unionists attempted to break.

Nevertheless, Quebec nationalists were forced to take note of the tremendous impact which the Canadian war effort had had on the country as a whole, including their own province. They could readily see that the participation they had so strenuously opposed had completely transformed Canada, in a way that went far beyond social and economic structures and reached deeply into mentalities. It was extremely painful for them to realize that the gap separating their French society from the rest of Canada and from the United States was becoming wider all the time. The various elites who held power in government, the Church, the universities, the media, and even in business felt themselves unable to face the task of planning and executing the massive catch-up operation that was clearly required. Their reaction was to cling more rigidly than ever to the traditional forms of organization and leadership and to stifle every attempt at critical self-examination.

Among the various effects of the war effort, two were particularly important for the future of French Quebec. The first was that after having marshalled vast human, financial, and material resources for military purposes, governments everywhere found themselves with unprecedented possibilities of intervention in the economy and in society in general. The other consequence of the war effort was that it accelerated the movement of population from the countryside into cities and towns. In Quebec this migration threatened the established order, which rested to a very large degree on control of parliamentary and public institutions by interests that were closely identified with agriculture and rural life. The perpetuation of conservative values was ensured by means of an electoral system which openly maintained a serious underrepresentation of city dwellers.

The scope of the ideological collapse threatening French Quebec was brought to the edge of consciousness with the gradual return to a peacetime economy subject to the ups and downs of the business cycle. The steps taken by federal authorities to prevent the recurrence of a crisis such as the Great Depression played a key role in this respect. Income redistribution through unemployment insurance and family allowances, which seek to sustain consumer demand and stabilize industrial production, forced French Quebec to take stock of the task of modernization which it had to set for itself.

It was at this point that French elites began to suspect that the political ideas prevalent in Quebec before the war had become almost totally irrelevant and had lost whatever hold they might have had over the population. The manner in which traditional elites had managed to harmonize North American capitalism with the social doctrines of the Catholic Church and with the national sentiment of French Quebec no longer met the very serious problems raised by accelerating industrialization and massive urbanization, by the progressive deterioration of the rural economy, and by the rapid expansion of federal powers and initiatives. Quebec society, particularly that part which still clung to traditional values, was thrown into a state of confusion and helplessness never experienced before. The cultural and religious foundations of French Quebec seemed to be disintegrating.

The ten years between the stock market crash of 1929 and the Second World War had been a period of stormy debates over various possible ways of reorganizing the economy, which as it happened was completely outside French control and management. The most widely held view was that the worst abuses of capitalism and of economic liberalism should be tempered by having the major organizations of society, including private companies and labour unions, participate in the formulation of government policy. There was a general desire to ensure the highest possible degree of social unity and solidarity by means of widespread consultations from the top down, according to a model already applied within the Catholic Church in Quebec. However, no real attempt was ever made to incorporate such a practice into official procedures by means of constitutional or institutional reform. The idea remained a pious wish for most people, except for a powerful minority of intellectuals who admired the corporatist model which had theoretically been implemented in Fascist Italy and who saw Mussolini as a rampart against communism and socialism as well as against the worst abuses of the capitalist economy.

Parallel to this movement, there were more practical attempts to bring about a greater measure of popular control over economic development in the province and to put an end to economic exploitation by various monopolies, particularly in electricity. There were also numerous campaigns to promote a better understanding of economics and management. While these preoccupations may have anticipated the nationalism of a subsequent period, they were not necessarily perceived in that light at the time: nationalism was then predominantly social and conservative in outlook.

The ideological ferment which had characterized the 1930s disappeared completely when the Union Nationale was returned to power after the war. Moving away from its previous state of agitation, public opinion now tended to polarize on the issue of centralization versus provincial autonomy, on the question of wider powers for the federal government as opposed to the extension of provincial jurisdiction in fiscal matters. The never-ending debate on the future of French Canada took a new turn as both levels of government began offering their own solutions and applying their own policies to resolve a problem which obviously was becoming more pressing all the time. Of course, the federal government's unusual eagerness to become involved in this situation was due to the fact that Prime Minister Louis Saint-Laurent himself was French Canadian and to the desire of the federal bureaucracy to expand its influence and authority.

French-speaking Liberals in Ottawa and Quebec saw cultural survival as dependent on a strong and modern economic base. They believed in a higher degree of participation in business life and integration into the economic system of Canada and the United States. With this in mind, federal authorities introduced various social security measures whose main effect would be to facilitate the transition from a rural and agricultural society to a new one which, while remaining inherently French, would be psychologically urban and industrial. From the Liberal point of view, nationalism was a reactionary ideology which favoured cultural and political isolationism, something that seemed inimical to the very notion of progress.

Such a conception of the future development of Quebec was not shared by Premier Duplessis. It was rejected out of hand by all those who supported the Union Nationale and participated in the exercise of power: the Catholic hierarchy, local elites throughout the province, all those involved in cultural occupations such as teaching, and those whose economic well-being was dependent in one way or another on provincial government spending. The political base supporting this edifice was the mass of voters whose livelihood was linked to agriculture. This was a class of people who had long been pampered by governments and who constituted the mainstay of French society in Quebec.

However, the kind of ideological control applied by provincial authorities had lost whatever vitality it may have shown in the past. It failed to offer a positive view of the future and it provided very little support for intellectual and speculative activities. Its most serious drawback was that it constituted a source of division by pitting one part of the population against another: those who lived from agriculture against those who lived from manufacturing and business. The rural mentality which pervaded official circles as well as the countryside was pitted against the urban mentality which dominated Montreal and was rapidly becoming more influential in various large towns across the province, such as Quebec City, Trois-Rivières, and Sherbrooke. French Quebec was thus a society which displayed crippling symptoms of division and conflict.

The traditional ideology, supported by the Catholic clergy, was incapable of integrating urbanization and industrialization into its system of thought, except in a negative fashion as

trends to be condemned and resisted. The Church had long
been aware that work in industrial organizations tended to
create new sets of values running counter to those which it
sought to perpetuate and which were closely tied to the
family, the community, and the Catholic faith. An economy
which requires that all obligations and responsibilities be
translated into cash payments will inevitably work to dissolve
the solidarity which individuals are expected to feel towards
one another. The overwhelming fear of the authorities, then,
was that the new liberal and industrial order would promote a
form of individualism which could undermine the historical
cohesiveness of the French in Quebec and imperil their cultural survival.

Accordingly, during this whole period, nationalists were
mainly concerned with the defence of the provincial government's constitutional jurisdiction against all federal encroachments which might produce undesirable changes. Provincial
autonomy became the principal ground on which Duplessis
and the various social classes supporting him chose to make
their stand.

The policy pursued by the Union Nationale on the home
front was to favour systematically those who were thought to
be supportive of the social order authorities had in mind. It
cynically excluded all others, whose ideas of progress and
freedom led towards the Liberal party. The exclusion was not
aimed solely at individuals: it affected entire social classes as
well as cities and ridings where the opposition happened to be
in a majority. Public funds constituted the main instrument of
discrimination.

In general fiscal policy, there was an overwhelming fear of
indebtedness, a holdover from the 1930s. So conservative was
the government in this respect that it was hindering the
province's economic growth. Instead of resorting to the bond
market to finance certain capital projects, Premier Duplessis
preferred making direct payments out of the provincial treasury. Consequently, taxpayers were forced to assume the
whole burden of public works such as roads and bridges, and

future generations, who were bound to derive considerable benefits from them, were exempt. This type of approach to public debt had the effect of keeping government spending at ridiculously low levels.

The provincial road network, particularly in the Montreal area, was in such a primitive state that it was stifling industrial development. Delays and added costs related to transportation became prohibitive with the growth of highway traffic. Towards 1960, the year the Union Nationale was voted out of office, farming too was being adversely affected, this at the very moment when it should have started looking at agribusiness and seeking improved access to markets and processing facilities. Conservatism was inexorably leading Quebec society towards internal collapse.

It is in the field of education that the prevailing ideology was most strongly expressed and where its subconscious desire to interrupt the course of history was most manifest. It is also there that the real nature of this moribund society was most clearly expressed.

The so-called classical colleges, which were private institutions administered and staffed by religious orders, were meant to train the young people who would eventually rise to the top of the social pyramid. Students enrolled immediately after completing grade school and received the French equivalent of a liberal arts education. These institutions provided the only possible access to higher education in the French language. It was through these *collèges classiques* and thanks to them that one could accede to the upper class. The clergy's strict supervision as well as the standardized character of the tuition were powerful contributing factors in preserving the cohesiveness of French society and instilling a sense of solidarity and social responsibility among its leadership.

Right up to 1960, provincial authorities still believed that elementary schooling met the basic needs of the rural population. Only in the larger cities did local school boards provide for secondary education, and this solely on their own initiative. These public schools gave no means of access to higher education. They offered only courses described in the terminology of that time as *terminal*. All they did was lead to subordinate jobs in business and industry.

The stubborn maintenance of an educational system that was so obviously obsolete and inadequate reflects the very limited ambitions of Quebec's traditional elites at that time. It tragically bespoke the constricted horizons and the cramped area which were felt to be theirs socially and economically. The preservation of this outdated educational system illustrated the very narrow range of occupations, professions, activities, and roles which authorities thought were desirable for the bulk of the French-speaking population.

The Catholic clergy played a leading part in determining the objectives pursued by educational institutions. The legislature and the government had practically abdicated every responsibility in this field and had assigned policy-making to two independent public bodies: the Catholic and the Protestant Committees of the department of public instruction, which acted independently of each other and in an entirely different spirit.

The shortcomings of the system were becoming apparent to an ever-increasing number of people. But it was difficult to call openly for reform without alerting and antagonizing the clergy, who wielded considerable political power and influence. Very few French-speaking people in Quebec dared link the deficiencies of the educational system with the Church. It remained for outsiders or for those who did not mind the resulting ostracism to raise the issue. English-speaking businessmen in Montreal often did so, with as much discretion as they could. However, one of the most explicit criticisms of the role of the Church belongs to a foreigner: André Siegfried, a member of the French Academy who made several trips to Canada between 1898 and 1935. He wrote abundantly about Canada's glowing prospects and about the troubled relations between English and French in this country. As a Protestant, he was quick to perceive the negative impact of the Catholic clergy on Quebec's development. In a book originally published in the mid-1930s, he wrote:

All teaching is under its control and its first preoccupation is to promote its own recruitment by taking for itself the best of its students. Its second preoccupation is to push aside whatever it fears, thereby sterilizing many seeds which otherwise might have usefully prospered. Its third preoccupation is to render impossible whatever is being done without its participation. We must acknowledge that it has not been able to provide the French-Canadian people with the kind of technical education that would have allowed them to claim their rightful place in the economic structure of the country. Excellent in the liberal professions, French Canadians generally remain outside the realm of industrial development: in the factories, management is English or American while the labour force is French.[1]

A surprising anomaly in this situation was the ease with which one could get around the deficiencies of the French educational system. This could be done by enrolling in English-language Catholic schools, which happened to be following Canadian and American models. This was the solution most favoured by those who wished for themselves or for their children to escape the stifling atmosphere of French society, who wanted broader professional horizons than those they were currently being offered, who felt imprisoned in a class system which had lost all creative spirit, or who saw in English education the only way of ensuring their success and prosperity.

Strangely enough, neither political nor religious authorities reacted to this disaffection for traditional values or to the drain on the most dynamic elements of their own society. Indeed, there was even some satisfaction in the fact that potential troublemakers chose symbolic exile instead of expressing their discontent by challenging official policies and disturbing the established order.

---

1. André Siegfried, Le Canada, puissance internationale (Paris: Librairie Armand Colin, 1956), 6th edition, p. 231 (author's translation).

The primary concern of the French establishment during the postwar period was to fence in the space occupied by its own society—its mental and cultural space and, if possible, its political and economic space as well. It was as if they expected the very essence of the French-Canadian nation to thrive in a closed and antiseptic atmosphere, protected against dangerous foreign influences likely to sway it from the historical and mystical vision that was supposed to guide it.

A majority of the people living at that time acted as if they feared becoming other than what they were. They clung desperately to reassuring pictures of a golden age somewhere in the past. In order to dispel the fear of a future that could not even be imagined, social and political controls became even more constricting. Every area of life which provincial authorities could act upon was affected by a tyrannical supervision aimed at preserving and sustaining ideological orthodoxy. At stake were the social structures and the roles inherited from the past.

The classical description of the political doctrine that held sway until the end of the Duplessis regime can be found in a sermon preached by Msgr. Louis-Adolphe Paquet of Laval University in 1902 on the occasion of Saint-Jean-Baptiste Day. The description of the role and the aptitudes of French Canadians, of their relations with English Canadians, is so naïve and grotesque that it is often quoted in anthologies and historical texts. But it still affords a good description of the basic ideas to which political speeches and patriotic exhortations were referring until about the late 1950s.

We are not merely a civilized race, we are the pioneers of civilization; we are not merely a religious people, we are the very messengers of the idea of religion. Our calling is not so much to handle capital as to weigh ideas; it is not so much to light the fires of factories as to make the light of religion and intellect shine as widely as possible. While our rivals may claim hegemony over industry and finance in a struggle that is no doubt courteous, we would rather compete on questions of doctrine; the laurels we seek are evangelical ones.[2]

In addition to the necessity of maintaining the close union of Church and state, contemporary thinking believed in the obligation to respect the terms of Confederation whereby the two founding nations should coexist peacefully and ensure the political stability of the country. This view rested in turn on the historical assumption that each partner had been given a vocation conforming to its aptitudes and interests. The English-speaking community occupied the domain of industry and finance and was said to be moved mainly by economic considerations. The French, on the other hand, would willingly remain a rural society steeped in religion and cultural pursuits.

One of the foremost objectives of Duplessis's government was therefore to compel observance of the terms of the federal pact. The Union Nationale eagerly welcomed Canadian firms wishing to invest in the province's natural resources and to make use of its abundant and docile labour supply. There was no thought of arousing popular sentiment for greater participation in local development. However, both party and government remained unyielding on all questions even remotely related to provincial autonomy and the federal system.

In 1954, with these ideas in mind, Duplessis abruptly moved to counter the federal government's tightening monopoly of the country's fiscal resources and its attempts to impose its own ideas of social and economic development on the provinces. He announced that his government would levy a new tax on personal and corporate incomes. It was, at the time, a move that was bound to draw a great deal of opposition and which constituted a grave political risk. However, the premier felt this was the only way to ensure his government's freedom of action in all areas deemed essential for the cultural security

2. Quoted by Robert Rumilly in *Histoire de la Province de Québec* (Montréal: Editions Bernard Valiquette), 10: 120–21 (author's translation).

of French Quebec. As he correctly anticipated, he received widespread popular support across the province for his defiance of federal power. Prime Minister Louis Saint-Laurent was forced to accept what turned out to be only the first step in a gradual expansion of the province's fiscal independence over the next twenty-five years.

A few years later, acting on the same principles, the Quebec government refused to participate in a hospital-insurance scheme put forward by federal authorities and which was to be financed jointly by the two levels of government. In this specific case, Duplessis opposed bureaucratic encroachments on Quebec institutions. It so happened that the vast majority of hospitals in the province were owned and staffed by religious orders, as was the school system. The federal proposal was thought to be dangerous because it undermined the close union between Church and state which Quebec was defending against modern trends to secularization. In the interest of sound financial management, Ottawa was making its contribution conditional on the complete separation of the hospitals from the religious orders that owned them; in other words they were to be incorporated separately. The provincial government replied this was an unwarranted intrusion into the organization of Quebec society. It flatly rejected the idea that hospital accounts should be subject to federal audits. As a result the federal plan was not implemented in Quebec even though Quebecers were unavoidably taxed to pay for hospital services in the other provinces which they themselves were not receiving.

Another aspect of federal action was that it tended to introduce into Quebec's political system bureaucratic procedures and standards of financial accountability incompatible with the personalized relations which government authorities maintained with religious, academic, and economic elites as well as with the innumerable village notables across the province. Political power perpetuated itself by means of favours granted and constraints imposed on those who benefited in any way from the largesse of the state. The archaic society to which Duplessis and the Union Nationale were attached could not survive after accepting a type of public administration which used objective and impartial standards in its dealings with persons and corporations.

As might be expected, this paternalistic type of administration came to be known as *duplessisme*. The word served to describe the corruption of the social and personal bonds which people in traditional societies have towards one another. In Quebec's postwar situation, when the pressures for change were building up, *duplessisme* was aberrant and anachronistic.

Practically all payments made out of the public treasury to hospitals, classical colleges, welfare organizations, and homes for the aged and for orphans were of a discretionary nature. They usually gave rise to comical pseudo-events when the director of some social institution, or the religious order responsible for it, formulated an urgent and dramatic plea for help to public authorities who then responded with theatrical generosity and self-serving publicity.

The state's relations with individuals and business firms were of the same character. The government had not set up a professional and independent civil service, so its administrative apparatus was easily confused with the party in power. Generally, ministers of the crown, members of the legislature, and political organizers did their best to make up for the administrative deficiencies of the state, which they were collectively responsible for in the first place. They were all very busy dispensing official patronage according to their individual lights and inclinations, to their personal interests and those of their party, and to the requirements of the social order they had in mind.

For the major part of Duplessis's long stay in office, the parliamentary opposition, which comprised the provincial Liberal party and in the mid-1940s the very nationalist Bloc Populaire, seemed incapable of staging a permanent breakthrough in rural areas, which remained loyal to the Union Nationale. Only in the cities could these two parties hold their own. Political conformity was indeed so repressive that the real and effective opposition was located outside parliamentary institutions and therefore tended to assume the character of a social revolt.

During those years, the labour movement was the mainstay of resistance against the Duplessis government. As the bearers of modern urban values deriving from industrial work, trade unions represented a disruptive element because of their social and economic demands, and because of the struggle they waged against large Canadian and American corporations. These corporations supported the government in its attempts to stave off reform, in exchange for legal and police assistance in major confrontations with labour.

The asbestos strike of 1949 marked the beginning of a long and bitter fight against *duplessisme* and crippling traditionalism. However, it is important to note in this respect that success became possible largely because of the ideological cracks that were appearing within the Catholic hierarchy, where a few influential persons had already perceived that the urban mentality would soon prevail over the rural one and eventually rule the province. Such figures as Msgr. Joseph Charbonneau, archbishop of Montreal, and the Rev. Georges-Henri Lévesque and Abbé Gérard Dion, both professors at Laval University, provided the anti-Duplessis resistance with a kind of legitimacy, so to speak, which helped to restrain the harshest and most repressive aspects of government policy.

For a long time the political and labour opposition remained too weak to overthrow the Union Nationale. The party continued to thrive because a substantial proportion of the population had given up on political action and had given in to feelings of powerlessness and even acquiescence in the face of official corruption. The very long moratorium on meaningful public debate after the Second World War paralysed the initiative of various organized groups who might otherwise have joined in support of the labour movement; it encouraged apathy and noninvolvement.

Most people were passively and patiently waiting for Duplessis to retire and transmit power to a successor no doubt handpicked by himself. But he died suddenly in office in September 1959, to the great relief of everyone except for a few close and loyal friends. He had long outlived his usefulness. His successor, Paul Sauvé, around whom the party spontaneously rallied, lived for only three months in office. During that brief time, he attempted to do away with the spirit of the old regime by launching a civil service reform and re-establishing a dynamic discussion of public affairs. The word he used most frequently and which helped him gain the required credibility at this critical juncture of Quebec history was "henceforth." After his death, Antonio Barrette took over and pushed on with reform. However, the basic philosophy of the Union Nationale, which still had not had sufficient time to evolve, was by then thoroughly discredited with the voters. Moreover, internal wrangling and divisions made the party unsuited for power. It went down to defeat in the general elections of June 1960.

Suddenly the old order had collapsed. Urban and industrial interests superseded the rural and agricultural bias which for more than a hundred years had been the foundation of French Canada's economic and social existence. The clergy's ability to shape collective destiny faded very swiftly. Almost from one day to the next, the nationalism which had sustained Quebec politics became reprehensible and reactionary. A yearning for freedom and modernity swept over the province.

The Quiet Revolution

When the provincial Liberals led by Jean Lesage took power in 1960 they were resolutely antinationalist. In their minds nationalism was closely identified with the stagnant Duplessis regime and they saw it as standing in the way of economic growth, the exercise of personal rights, and even honest and efficient government. According to them, it was essentially a conservative movement or reflex promoting strict cultural isolation in order to forestall unwelcome social changes.

This way of seeing things was undoubtedly the product of long years of political opposition and of official discrimination on the part of the Union Nationale government. But it can also be attributed to the character of the Liberal organization at that time and to the way in which it approached political action in Ottawa and Quebec.

The Liberal party of that period had hardly any stable and permanent structure. However, it did have a national organization with a number of provincial sections exhibiting varying degrees of effectiveness. It was supposed to be one big happy political family and there was no formal distinction between the two levels of political action. Nevertheless, the main centre of interest lay in the federal government and it was expected that provincial sections, particularly if they happened to be in power, would give active support to the federal party and its goals.

The Liberals constituted the party of national integration during the twentieth century as the Conservatives had in the nineteenth. They have worked to unite as closely as possible the various regions of the country and to overcome the centrifugal forces tending to disrupt the Canadian system.

This policy, conceived primarily with the interests of English Canada in mind, had its counterpart for French Canada. The government of Quebec was considered a subordinate administration whose powers and responsibilities were relatively limited. It was concerned solely with what one might call the internal affairs of the French-speaking population. The promotion of French minority interests within Canada was expected to take place at the federal level. It was in Ottawa that the major decisions affecting relations between the so-called founding nations of Canada were to be taken.

In Quebec, the very idea of change, which had already become suspect, gave rise to severe political anxiety because of two factors associated with the war effort. One was the accelerating industrialization and modernization of Quebec and the other was the expansion of the federal government's tax revenues, which vastly increased its interventionist capacities and its political leverage. The federal Liberals, led by Louis Saint-Laurent, confidently believed that the best solution for Quebec lay in closer integration with the rest of Canada. They categorically rejected the idea that this might prove dangerous for French cultural survival. In fact, the Liberals felt that the real danger lay in maintaining the isolation which the Duplessis and the Union Nationale were imposing on the province.

In accordance with this way of thinking, the provincial Liberals were sustained and led during their lean years in opposition by members of the federal wing. In 1952 Georges Lapalme gave up a seat in the House of Commons to take over the provincial party. He was replaced in 1958 by Jean Lesage, a former minister of Indian affairs in the Saint-Laurent government. Both came to provincial politics with the idea of asserting an order of intergovernment relations which they considered natural and desirable.

When they took power in 1960, the victorious Liberals did not think in terms of a social system providing protection and guidance for everyone. They gave priority to individualism and to the rights which the previous regime had purposely eroded.

The new government was committed to the principles of classical liberalism, in other words, to the very principles which a society dedicated to the safeguard of national and of family values had systematically pushed aside in the name of a stifling concept of group solidarity. The liberation associated with the defeat of the Union Nationale was that of individuals against social constraints which weighed too heavily upon them.

All the discretionary and arbitrary practices of the previous administration came under attack. The ultimate goal was to make all public services and social benefits available to everyone on an egalitarian basis. A spectacular public inquiry presided over by Judge Elie Salvas of the Quebec Superior Court looked into the abuses of pork-barrel politics and condemned the corruption attributed to the Union Nationale. Expectations were that the Salvas Report would have such an exemplary value as to accelerate the process of modernization that the Liberals had in mind.

However, the winds of change blew strongest in the field of education. A reform of the school system had been initiated in 1959 by the Union Nationale under Paul Sauvé. A system of grants was established to encourage local and regional school boards to improve their curricula and to incite them to counteract the strong propensity of the student population to drop out of school at a relatively early age. It was a rather timid and limited reform which hardly dealt with the contents of the educational system or with its philosophy. The clergy and the Church remained in firm control through the Catholic Committee of the department of public instruction.

It was Paul Gérin-Lajoie, the Liberal minister responsible for education, who energetically pushed for further and more aggressive changes. The catch phrase he used was "democratization of education." The reform was designed to benefit individuals first of all and then society, in accordance with the order of priorities which the Liberals had established and in which they firmly believed.

This was, in effect, an attack on the old social order with its class distinctions which, for historical reasons proper to Quebec, rested on education rather than on wealth. The entire population was expected to benefit from the greater accessibility of education at all levels. Children were to be offered more social mobility and broader professional opportunities than any previous generation had known. The initial effort concentrated on expansion of the high-school network to cover rural areas and smaller towns across the province, and later on establishment of a new network of junior colleges which would prepare students for university faculties. At the same time, tuition fees were done away with at pre-university levels.

Educational programs were also modified to reflect the government's democratic preoccupations. Instead of offering a uniform curriculum to all students as had been done until then, authorities began to make allowances for variations in personal aptitudes and inclinations, just as they accepted the fact that there could be great differences in learning speeds. Ideally, the new system was designed to encourage the maximum development of each child's capabilities, which had never been seen in Quebec as part of the state's responsibilities.

These ideas pertaining to the preeminence of the individual in society, as applied to the educational system, were not mere pedagogical abstractions. They reflected the delayed acceptance of an economy linked to industry and city life, with all its requirements for social organization and the training of individuals. It is not surprising therefore that school curricula should also have been adapted to the needs of many categories of employers who demanded longer periods of schooling, even in junior or menial jobs.

The effects of educational reform, however, were not limited to overturning traditional values as they happened to be expressed by Duplessis and the Union Nationale. Reform laid the groundwork for a subsequent assault on the domain historically occupied by the English-speaking minority in Quebec: the managerial and executive jobs in large Canadian corporations with head offices or important operations in Montreal.

Introducing democratic ideals into the educational system had the natural consequence of forcing a greater measure of democracy upon the industrial society for which students were being prepared. At that point it was no longer possible to accept, as had been done for over two hundred years, a situation whereby English and French in Canada followed different callings, the first to the management of the national economy, and the second to professional or agricultural occupations within a marginal and static society turned in upon itself. The reformed educational system encouraged the French majority in the province to take possession of the cities in a way that had never really been imagined before. Without it being explicitly stated, this meant taking possession of the economy that had created these cities and now sustained them.

French-Canadian society began spilling over its old psychological boundaries into new spaces, the very ones it had long neglected and abandoned to others. This movement was basically that of individuals who were being educated and mentally prepared for modern careers and occupations. There was no thought yet about a conquest to be achieved by society as a whole after its members had been mobilized to that end, or through the legislative and administrative intervention of the state, which had the power to expand French economic territory at the expense of the English. These ideas were practically unknown during the early stages of the Quiet Revolution. Nevertheless, the urban attitudes encouraged by educational reform helped trigger a new upsurge of nationalist sentiment.

The role of the state in the economy was meant to be strictly supportive. This was the mission given to the General Investment Corporation, which after receiving government seed money was supposed to channel private savings into forms of investment beneficial to Quebec. In 1962, when Natural Resources Minister René Lévesque persuaded the cabinet to nationalize private power companies, he thought Hydro-Quebec could become an active agent of industrial development by means of preferential rates for certain industries and for certain areas of the province. He never had sufficient authority, however, to rally his colleagues to his point of view or to impose it on Hydro-Quebec itself. The expanding Crown corporation rapidly became an industrial giant, a sort of state within a state which the government is still unable to bend to its will.

Nationalization of electricity in 1962 was the pretext for a general election called to provide the government with the necessary mandate. The campaign was waged on the slogan *Maîtres chez nous*, "Masters in our own house," which alluded to the stormy debates that had taken place some thirty years earlier on the possibility of ending the exploitation of the so-called electricity trusts. But, in spite of the support which the government sought for the takeover of private power companies, its program of economic development called for reliance on private enterprise rather than on any notion of direct state intervention. The fact that the overwhelming majority of large and medium-sized firms were staffed by English-speaking people and that English was the language of their administration had not yet intruded on the political awareness of voters and politicians. The state was to remain a minor instrument in the task of modernization that was to be taken on. Everyone believed that the change in mentalities brought on by the defeat of the Union Nationale would be enough to propel the province forward. Nationalization of electricity was presented as an exceptional step.

As it turned out, the liberal ideology of personal initiative and free enterprise did not represent for very long the mainstream of the Quiet Revolution. Quebec politics took a new and unforeseen turn as a result of developments taking place in conjunction with educational reform, the escalation of public spending, and a new-found prosperity.

What seems to characterize this recent period of Quebec's history is the appearance for the first time of a strong government, a strong state, concentrating within itself the expectations of the French-speaking population and subsequently assuming the task of inspiring and promoting nationalist sentiment. This was a highly significant development.

Historically, the state in Quebec had always been weak. Its resources and its influence on society as a whole were limited. Until the Quiet Revolution, the state had no real independence or autonomy such as it has now acquired thanks to its powerful bureaucracy. It was entirely under the control of the legislature and of the cabinet. Indeed, it was the cabinet that constituted the real focus of converging interests such as the Catholic Church, agricultural producers, big business, commerce, various pressure groups, and all others who had access to power.

The establishment of a powerful state was certainly not among the plans which the Liberal party had prepared for the day when it would take over the government. On the contrary, it shared in the widely felt fear of statism. But little by little and without quite being aware of it, the new administration was pushed forward by the momentum of the reforms it had initiated. The modernization of Quebec society and the expansion of social security brought about a rapid increase in public spending and in the number of civil servants. The bureaucracy's thirst for power grew proportionately.

The first large bureaucratic empire to take shape within the provincial government was set up to implement reform of the educational system. As the manpower and the material resources brought together for this purpose were far in excess of actual needs, it soon became apparent that this was not only a new way of exercising power but a new form of power altogether. The tasks assumed by the bureaucracy were not concerned solely with administration and planning. They were at times highly political in the sense that civil servants were actively engaged in the transformation of mentalities and expectations. They were involved in a form of social engineering that was unprecedented in the Quebec government.

For the first time in Quebec's history, at least since the French Regime, the state was actually taking charge of society. In the field of education, it began determining the needs of the population and taking whatever steps were necessary to meet them. It stopped being dependent for these functions on associates such as the Catholic clergy and Church, and stopped allowing local school boards a free rein in setting their own policies. It was in these circumstances that the state began a relatively rapid transformation which ultimately left most institutions and groups in Quebec society with very little autonomy. Retrospectively, the state's tendency to assume an ever-broadening range of responsibilities offered an astonishing contrast with the liberalism professed at that time by the people who wielded political authority.

The person who engineered this transformation in the role of the state was Paul Gérin-Lajoie, the minister responsible for educational reform. The new department of education, which in 1964 replaced the autonomous department of public instruction, was set up with a chain of command and levels of decision-making resembling those of General Motors and other large U.S. corporations. Gérin Lajoie was the first member of the provincial government to rely systematically on computers as instruments of management. These innovations brought fundamental changes to the character of public administration in Quebec.

His behaviour as minister provides valuable insight into the nature of the transformations he effected. In the numerous political crises which unavoidably cropped up during the enterprising Lesage administration, Gérin-Lajoie consistently displayed his solidarity with the advisers and civil servants under his command rather than with his colleagues in the cabinet. This was the real reason for the irresistible political influence he wielded at the time and which allowed him to obtain for his department a major share of the provincial budget in spite of the agonized protests of other cabinet members. He was paternalistic in his demeanour and he saw himself as a great public administrator rather than as a spokesman for the popular will. It was the kind of image which some of his colleagues like René Lévesque and Eric Kierans also tried to project.

It was perhaps a natural thing to do at a time when reforms were concerned with efficiency, enlightenment, impartiality, and social justice. Such a trait was encouraged by the mood of the times, which tended to throw discredit on any politician who was too familiar with the people or who attempted to flatter them. This type of relationship was highly suspect because it was associated with the spirit of Premier Duplessis and the old Union Nationale government. It helps to explain the arrogance which came to be popularly attributed to the provincial Liberals and which helped precipitate their downfall in 1966.

The idea of a strong and active state, as new and revolutionary as it seemed at the time, rapidly took hold among all those who were involved in political activities, not to mention those who staffed the public service. While Paul Gérin-Lajoie had shaped a new role for the state and had demonstrated its effectiveness, it was another person who provided the ideological justification for this new concept and who linked it with an increasingly pervasive and aggressive form of nationalism. This was Claude Morin; at the time he was discreetly acting as adviser to Premier Lesage on matters pertaining to federal-provincial relations. He later became deputy minister of intergovernmental affairs and played a similar role with three other premiers: Daniel Johnson, Jean-Jacques Bertrand, and Robert Bourassa. In 1976, some time after leaving the public service, he was elected to the National Assembly as a member of the Parti Québécois. On becoming minister of intergovernmental affairs in René Lévesque's government he completed the passage from the bureaucracy to politics, which is exactly the reverse of what Gérin-Lajoie's behaviour had suggested earlier.

The sudden expansion of state power was a catalyst lending credibility to a number of ideas which had been around for a long time but had never seemed particularly relevant. No doubt the most important one was the view that Quebec represents the political centre of French Canada and that this province must do everything it can to preserve and develop its own characteristics. On many occasions since Confederation, heads of the Quebec government had expressed such a view as they tried to hold their own against the pressures exerted by the federal government. But it was merely a sentimental statement that could not yet be translated into a program.

A more recent but equally powerful idea was that the government should be ultimately responsible for the welfare of everyone in the province. For quite some time already, the needs of the population had exceeded the limited scope of the various social services which religious orders had traditionally offered. Under Duplessis this situation had given rise to an outrageous increase in political patronage and to a paralysing intervention by elected members of the legislature in the day-to-day administration of the government. By the time of the Quiet Revolution in 1960, reform had become urgent. But the Liberals had not yet formulated a general philosophy or the guiding principles that would sustain government action. This is exactly what Claude Morin provided when he was adviser to successive premiers.

One of his most important assignments was drafting the briefs which Quebec submitted to the numerous federal-provincial conferences which were then coming to play an extremely important role in the federal system. These documents, as might be expected, concentrated mainly on policy differences between Quebec and Ottawa—that is, on the conflictual aspect of their relations. In this respect, one of the most contentious points between the two levels of government concerned federal expenditures in areas lying within the constitutional jurisdiction of the provinces. On many occasions, the Quebec government complained that its spending priorities and long-range plans were constantly being upset by untimely and unpredictable offers by federal authorities which they could not afford to turn down. These usually took the form of shared-cost programs in such areas as health, social aid, education, and municipal affairs.

In this climate of intergovernmental tension, Claude Morin gradually formulated the political point of view according to which only the government of Quebec is able to ensure the social and economic development of the French-Canadian nation and consequently it should enjoy all the fiscal and constitutional powers necessary for this purpose.

The ground covered by these claims was quite extensive and became more so as the Quebec government organized its thoughts on the subject. After having asserted that no federal initiative could take precedence over its own jurisdiction in education, welfare, health, and urban affairs, the Quebec government began asserting the right to sign agreements with foreign countries and international organizations on any matter that came within its constitutional authority. It also began criticizing the mandate given to such federal bodies as the Central Mortgage and Housing Corporation and Radio-Canada.

Imperceptibly and without debate on the question outside the context of federal-provincial wrangling over constitutional issues, the idea of the welfare state rapidly took hold. Public opinion spontaneously came to see it as the only answer to the problems of social organization which were becoming crucial at that time. As the welfare state took shape, it abolished the political differences between the Liberal party and the Union Nationale, both of which became vocal supporters of social-democracy. However, new sources of political tension became manifest. The growth of bureaucratic power in Quebec encouraged estrangement from Ottawa and the rest of Canada.

Thus the welfare state came to be the political expression of a new form of nationalism which was closely linked with the modernization policies launched by the Lesage government. The individualism which the Quiet Revolution had been promoting in its early days in reaction to the stifling conformity imposed by the Duplessis regime gave way to a new form of egalitarianism. It was defined as the right of everyone to share equally in the largesse of the state.

By turning its back on classical liberalism, which for a brief period had seemed to be taking hold, Quebec reverted to a type of social control and leadership which were largely patterned on the role which the Catholic clergy had taken on during the 100-year period between Confederation and the Quiet Revolution. From the early 1960s on, the historical role of the clergy was assumed by a new elite: the state bureaucracy.

It soon showed itself to be extremely powerful and enterprising. The state bureaucracy quickly appropriated for its

own benefit whatever nationalist sentiments the French population still harboured because of its weak economic situation
and its minority position within the federal system. Nationalism was invoked to check the invasion of a rival force, that of
the federal bureaucracy, which had a head start of many years
on its provincial counterpart. Nationalism provided the justification needed by the provincial bureaucracy for the tight
control it was extending over Quebec society at the expense
of the Church and local government. Finally, nationalism
proved useful in mobilizing the population to support the process of modernization, which was both urgent and difficult.

The guerilla war waged against the federal government
sought to discredit it in the eyes of French voters. This was
relatively easy while John Diefenbaker was prime minister.
He had very little understanding of the situation in Quebec
and had few able or trustworthy advisers to inform him. In
addition, the federal public service was overwhelmingly
English-speaking and extraordinarily accident-prone in its
dealings with French-speaking people.

The confrontation took on a new dimension when Lester
Pearson became prime minister in 1963. A strong French
presence in the new Liberal government in Ottawa helped
compensate for the ineptitude of the federal civil service and
contributed enormously to drawing a larger number of French-
speaking people to its ranks. However, French-speaking members of Parliament and civil servants naturally took up the
defence of federal institutions against the political attacks
launched by their counterparts in Quebec City. They revived
the old Liberal idea according to which French cultural survival could be ensured only by means of an aggressive presence
within federal institutions; withdrawal within Fortress Quebec was believed to be culturally suicidal. This was the first
manifestation of French Power which later came to be associated with Pierre Trudeau.

Given the very close and assiduous contacts which politicians and civil servants usually maintain with one another,
the clash between the two giant bureaucracies had profound
repercussions on the inner workings of the Liberal party. It

had always been a large political family recruiting workers and personnel from both the federal and provincial scenes; it now began to show serious signs of strain. Under heavy pressure from Quebec nationalists, it eventually had to accept a separation reflecting that between the two levels of government. The question was originally raised by René Lévesque: how can the party retain the confidence of the public when from one side of its mouth it is preaching provincial autonomy and from the other it is committed to the centralization of Canadian institutions?

This inner contradiction, which had been easily accepted until then, suddenly became unbearable. Political involvement in the 1960s became so intense that it was no longer possible to cope with competing objectives within a single party. Accordingly the federal and the Quebec wings of the Liberal party went their separate ways. While their members were still largely made up of the same people, their leaders became closely identified with the institutions and the vested interests attached to each level of government. In other words, the rivalry went beyond bureaucracy and became institutional and governmental.

Once the party split had been confirmed in 1965, the confrontation became even more intense. Quebec, with its French-speaking civil service, managed to score several gains against Ottawa, particularly in tax-sharing and in the administrative standards incorporated into shared-cost programs. However, the province was powerless to do anything about the principles and the structures governing its relations with Ottawa. It proved impossible to obtain constitutional concessions to reflect a change in the balance of power between the two orders of government. Only limited headway could be made against Ottawa.

However, there was total victory over the Catholic Church. Acceptance of the federal hospital-insurance plan in 1960 launched an irreversible trend towards secularization of all social institutions administered by the clergy. The high point in this process came in 1964 with the establishment of a true department of education under the control of the cabinet and legislature. It was a momentous event in Quebec in the sense that it represented a changing of the guard among the ruling elites of French society.

It is noteworthy that the Church offered very little resistance to the termination of its historical role in Quebec. There are very few countries where the passage from clericalism to a real separation of Church and state has been achieved with so much tact on the part of the government and accepted with so little acrimony by the clergy. However, this development was inevitable and it obviously came in response to the popular will, which was increasingly manifest. In any event, the Church no longer had the human and material resources to maintain its historical presence and meet the ever-growing needs of the population. The undoubted perceptiveness of the clergy on this occasion was reinforced by the fact that this transfer of power was long overdue.

Nevertheless, one can understand the reasons causing the Church to fear the emergence of powerful state institutions which would challenge its preeminent role and divert to their own ends the allegiance of the population. The clergy had assumed in Quebec many functions which in other countries had long been taken over by public authorities, such as the registers of births, marriages, and deaths, as well as the educational system. Therefore, the past influence of the Church cannot be attributed solely to the religious sentiment of the people; it was also derived from the powers and responsibilities which elsewhere had come to be assumed by the state. The expansion of government activity in many areas could be achieved only at its expense and this the Church had always known. It was so deeply rooted in Quebec that it was able, at this historical moment, to foresee the necessity of seeking a new role for itself and for the clergy.

The only rival for the newly discovered power of the state was the business community, whose leadership was mainly in the hands of an Anglo-Protestant elite. But no one in the party or in the government had any intention of challenging it overtly. There was general recognition of the vital importance of business and of the role played by the English-speaking minority in the province. Nevertheless, the Liberals did make certain moves which might retrospectively be interpreted as subconscious displays of animosity. The most important one in this regard was the reform of the Election Act, which was ostensibly intended to improve political morality.

The abuses perpetrated by the Union Nationale during its long years in power had left bitter memories among many Liberals. They attributed their prolonged stay in opposition to the distortion of electoral processes resulting from the multi-million-dollar slush fund accumulated by the governing party. It was constantly being replenished by contributions from large companies, contractors, and professionals who had regular dealings with the provincial government. The fund gave the Union Nationale an almost insurmountable advantage at election time. The situation was all the more galling in that the federal wing of the Liberal party not only withheld any financial assistance but had contracted some sort of non-aggression pact with the Union Nationale.

The first amendments to the Election Act had the effect of giving members of the legislature a greater measure of independence from traditional sources of funding. The new law provided for the reimbursement of electoral expenditures to candidates obtaining more than a certain percentage of the vote. It also imposed a ceiling on election spending. The idea was to reduce the risk of corruption among elected officials. Psychologically, the reforms served to reinforce the self-satisfaction and the virtuous feelings of politicians. In this manner, the odium of corruption and graft was transferred to the shoulders of businessmen and private enterprise who supposedly influenced public policy for selfish ends. The effect of the protracted debates on electoral reform was to widen the gulf separating the French-speaking population from large Canadian corporations whose management was predominantly English-speaking. The law helped neutralize powerful vested interests which might have stood in the way of the expanding power of politicians and bureaucrats.

Participation of English-speaking businessmen in public affairs was already on the wane. Bureaucratic intervention in education, health, and welfare had very nearly the same consequences for them as for the Catholic clergy: they were progressively pushed aside from the managerial responsibilities they had always assumed as a matter of course in various community services. The reforms brought to the Election Act, and especially some of their underlying motivation, deepened the isolation of the business community. By way of consequence, big business was led to identify more and more closely with federal power and to view political trends in Quebec as inimical to its own interests.

The neutralization of the business community was only one of many factors which allowed the provincial bureaucracy to dominate the entire political scene. The secularization of community institutions and the elimination of the Catholic clergy from practically every position of power represented another important transformation. However, bureaucratic power was most strengthened by the eagerness with which political parties and even the cabinet accepted its definition of the province's needs. Eventually, there was only one area that remained immune to its influence and that was the one covered by federal authority.

It was at this moment, impossible to pin down exactly in time, that the Quiet Revolution finally managed to bring about the internal unity of French society in Quebec. It succeeded in ending the division which had persisted for quite some time between the old rural society and the new urban one whose attitudes and values were now asserting themselves everywhere. The Quiet Revolution, therefore, completed the homogenization of French society, a process which had really started in the mid-1950s with the advent of television. In several ways, journalists and media played a key role in this last phase of Quebec's modernization: by vigorously denouncing the vestiges of the Duplessis regime, by preparing the population for a more active role on the part of the state, by spreading new ideas of progress and social organization, and, most of all, by promoting new forms of collective awareness.

The united and homogeneous society which emerged as a result of the Quiet Revolution gave unexpected resonance to the ideas expressed by the numerous celebrities who emerged in the media, in politics, and even in the public service. The nature of the audience had changed dramatically: it was now much more numerous and sensitive then it had been in the past. A relatively homogeneous mass had replaced the fragmented public of an earlier age.

This was, incidentally, the very situation that the media hoped for in order to expand their commercial operations. To maximize the impact of advertising they needed a homogenized and unified market rather than one that was broken down into different classes, mentalities, interests, and tastes. It was important in this respect to integrate the rural population into the consumer society that had already taken over the cities and larger towns. Reporters and media stars who defended the achievements of Jean Lesage and his government were unconscious participants in a vast movement that was levelling mentalities, introducing a new form of social conformity, and, at the same time, unifying the audience for advertising and the market for consumer goods. These were undeniably the key aspects of the modernization process with which the Quiet Revolution had become identified.

It gradually became clear that educational reform was going in a totally different direction than the one originally planned. Its movement was parallel to that of the consumer society. Instead of placing the individual at the very centre of pedagogical concerns and making the system operate for his benefit, the bureaucratic mind that had taken control substituted an entirely new objective. This was the schooling of large masses of students to meet the requirements of industry and of the economy in general.

Collective goals showed themselves to be far more attractive than the sum of individual ones. The philosophical liberalism which had been at the origin of the Quiet Revolution was, in fact, only a brief interlude in Quebec's political life. Inexorably imposing its will, there began to emerge a new force capable of maintaining a form of social control very similar to that of the Church in its method and its pervasive presence: this was the provincial bureaucracy.

The Créditiste Revolt

In the general elections of 18 June 1962, the Conservative government of John G. Diefenbaker, which had been elected four years earlier with a record majority, barely managed to hang on to power. It unexpectedly found itself in a minority in the House of Commons. The biggest surprise of that election, however, was the appearance for the first time in Quebec of the Créditiste phenomenon. Of the 75 members of Parliament allotted to this province, the Créditistes managed to elect 26, the Liberals 35, and the Conservatives 14.

The Diefenbaker government survived precariously until March of the following year, when the Créditistes joined with the opposition to bring it down. In the ensuing elections on 8 April 1963, the Créditistes elected only 20 members but they increased their share of the popular vote in Quebec from 25 to 30 per cent. Réal Caouette, their leader in Quebec, thereby displayed a political strength which had to be reckoned with.

These events caused consternation among federal Liberals, who were unable to understand why such a large proportion of voters in Quebec should support a third party which had never proved itself and which, to top it all, had been campaigning on an economic program that was behond human comprehension. The federal scene was profoundly perturbed for at least a dozen years by a political party whose efforts resulted in splitting the massive French vote on which the Liberals were counting to maintain themselves in power in Ottawa.

Oddly enough, those who seemed most concerned by the turn of events were the provincial Liberals in Quebec, as well as all those who supported the effort of modernization which already was being referred to as the Quiet Revolution. It was felt that the French version of Social Credit threatened not only the stability of Liberal rule in Ottawa but also, in some mysterious way, the very foundations of the modern society that was then emerging in Quebec. Apart from this philosophical anxiety, as it were, there was the more down-to-earth possibility of a Créditiste invasion of the provincial scene.

The prevailing feeling in some quarters was very close to panic. There was a widespread desire among the province's elites to crush this dangerous movement before it could take root. Thus, during the federal election campaign of April 1963, many leading personalities decided to do battle with the Créditistes in their own strongholds, the Lake St. John, Abitibi and Quebec City regions. Among them were René Lévesque, natural resources minister in the Lesage government, Jean Marchand, president of the Confederation of National Trade Unions, and Eric Kierans, president of the Montreal Stock Exchange. Premier Lesage himself made a few speeches urging the voters, in the interests of Quebec and of French Canada, to show confidence in Liberal leader Lester Pearson.

When Réal Caouette entered the House of Commons for the first time in 1962, he had been preaching the doctrine of Social Credit for a dozen years or so. He had crisscrossed the province in the company of Louis Even and Gilberte Côté-Mercier when the movement was still called l'Union des électeurs. At that time it had a pseudo-religious character: the prophecies of Our Lady of Fatima were intertwined with the financial theories of a retired British Army engineer, Major C. H. Douglas. The Créditistes had attempted a political breakthrough in 1956 when the provincial Liberals led by Georges Lapalme had proposed an alliance against the Union Nationale. The alliance proved fruitless and served only to cover the Liberals with ridicule.

Little by little Caouette dropped the mystical and religious ideas which his earlier associates had linked with Social Credit. He decided to confine himself to the political and economic theories of Major Douglas, which proposed the payment of a so-called social dividend as a way of boosting the population's purchasing power and bringing it into line with the country's productive capacity. This was the first step in the reforms which Social Credit was expected to bring about.

Another aspect of the program which the voters thought particularly attractive consisted in manipulating credit in such a way as to "render financially possible that which is materially feasible." According to Major Douglas, the population's purchasing power in the form of salaries, wages, and dividends was way below the production costs of all the goods and services available at a given time. This ever-widening gap was blamed on the banks and those whom Caouette usually referred to as "the sharks of high finance" who controlled credit for their own profit. This situation, which Caouette said was characteristic of contemporary capitalism, could be corrected only by applying the reforms put forth by Social Credit.

It is impossible to say precisely at what point the voters began to swing towards Social Credit. However, the trend may be partly explained by the rise in unemployment and the onset of inflationary pressures in the late 1950s and early 1960s. To thousands of workers who felt uprooted as a result of this situation, Social Credit appeared like a magical and comforting solution. This doctrine, which no one could properly explain to the faithful and which today arouses hardly any interest, seemed to be related to a question which had worried nationalists of an earlier period: how is it that money was so easily found for war but is not available for the unemployed in peacetime? However, while the nationalists were not inclined or never dared to question the economic system itself, the Créditistes did so in a manner so insistent and aggressive that it provoked the creation of a common political front against them.

In many respects Réal Caouette's career is similar to that of William Aberhart, who brought Social Credit to Alberta after the onset of the Great Depression in 1929. A schoolteacher and preacher, Aberhart founded the Prophetic Bible Institute in 1930 to sponsor his Sunday afternoon sermons on radio. As it turned out, these broadcasts were immensely popular. By 1932 Aberhart started incorporating political ideas into his religious themes. His influence grew by leaps and bounds, and when provincial elections were called in 1935 he decided to enter the fray. Against all expectations, his highly dedicated grass-roots organization swept him into office. He then made several attempts to apply Social Credit ideas but immediately came up against provisions of the British North America Act which gave exclusive jurisdiction over money and banking to the federal government. Alberta laws dealing with these topics were disallowed by the Supreme Court. Although the party was never able to implement its economic ideas, it remained in power in Alberta for thirty-six years, thanks to the prosperity that returned with wartime and to the discovery of immense oil and gas resources.

As Aberhart was the first politician in Canada to make use of radio as a political instrument, Caouette was the first to really understand the psychological impact of television. His skill in communicating ideas and feelings had been acquired not through preaching or teaching but through selling auto-mobiles in Rouyn-Noranda. He quickly became a political star, but he was totally ignored by the intellectual elite of Quebec, which was unaware of the power of television and of its uses. In fact, Caouette's hold on a large section of the public remained very strong in spite of the systematic opposition of all media, and long after his party had ceased being an effec-tive outlet for popular dissatisfaction. His good-naturedness and the comical way in which he could short-circuit logical sequences were imitated far and wide and helped change the style of political oratory in the French language in Quebec.

Just as Aberhart had done before him, Caouette demon-strated that a political party does not need corporate bagmen and contributions to elect its candidates and that it can rely on the commitment of its own supporters. Not only did he steal a march on the provincial Liberals engaged in electoral reform, but he showed that significant improvements are more likely to result from changes in mentalities than from legislation and bureaucratic regulations.

Créditistes in Quebec took note of Aberhart's failure to implement his economic views at the provincial level. Accordingly, Caouette chose to do battle at the federal level, where the constitutional authority to deal with credit, the monetary system, and the banks happened to be located. He did this at a time when nationalists had already started turning their backs on federal politics and when the provincial government was coming to be perceived as the only legitimate agent of social change in Quebec. It was a time when the very concept of federalism was beginning to be viewed with disfavour and suspicion. This helps to explain a general inability to grasp the movement's identification with nationalist sentiment and the key role it played in the province's subsequent political development. Its importance stems from the nature and the tone of the protest which it expressed for more than fifteen years.

The Créditistes were attacking not only abuses of the economic system but also, more or less consciously, the rationality behind it. This was the very aspect of Social Credit in Quebec which frightened the educated French middle class. In numerous speeches Caouette invited his listeners to dissociate themselves from an inadequate economic system because they had nothing to lose. This kind of call threatened to undermine the basic solidarity of French society.

He knew how to focus on the contradictions of the system so as to bring out the solutions proposed by his own party. In 1962 and 1963, when unemployment was particularly severe, he said over and over again to the large crowds that were coming to hear him: "They say Social Credit will bring inflation and that your money won't be worth anything. But this isn't a very strong argument when you consider that most of you don't have a cent in your pockets. They'll have to find something better with which to stop Social Credit!" This particular way of reasoning was quite new at the time and Caouette's success with it had considerable influence on all those who for one reason or another were challenging the existing social and economic order, whether separatist or extreme left-wing groups. Caouette created a new rhetoric which modified the tone and later the contents of political debates.

While John Diefenbaker was slowly losing control over the voters, the House of Commons, and even his own cabinet, federal Liberals were worried that their chances of coming to power might be compromised by the Créditiste breakthrough. Indeed, the feeling of panic was so prevalent in the party that leading personalities in Quebec were called to the rescue. To this end, Liberal leader Lester Pearson let it be understood that as head of a new government he would be ready to make major concessions to the historical demands of French Canada concerning linguistic equality and provincial autonomy.

One person who heeded the Liberal call was the president of the Montreal Stock Exchange, Eric Kierans. In what was still fractured French, he threw himself into the 1963 election campaign and went to the Lake St. John area to beef up business resistance to the blandishments of Social Credit. He tried to point out the optical illusions inherent in Créditiste interpretations of economic realities. According to Kierans, the control of the nation's interest rates along Social Credit lines would result in the centralization of economic authority in government, because private enterprise would necessarily have to obtain credit from federal civil servants. This concentration of economic power in the hands of the public service would eventually stifle private enterprise. Kierans thus sought to demonstrate the contradictory aspects of the Social Credit program, which called for an increase in government powers while strenuously opposing statism.

During the campaign the Liberals bought full-page ads in various Quebec newspapers reproducing the unfavourable comments of various Quebec personalities about the Social Credit program and the promises which its proponents were making to the voters. One of them was René Lévesque. Retrospectively, his comments seem somewhat naïve: "They're telling people that credit, money and dividends constitute an absolute and inexhaustible cure-all. Isn't it deceitful to promise people they will find work overnight?"[1] What Lévesque

---

1. *Le Devoir*, 2 April 1963 (author's translation).

did not quite understand was that the people whose views he was criticizing did hope for miracle solutions to their problems and that they had long stopped trusting people who claimed that improvements could come only in the very long run as a result of careful planning.

More significant was the quotation attributed to Jean Marchand, who was then president of the Confederation of National Trade Unions and who in 1965 joined the Liberals along with Pierre Trudeau and Gérard Pelletier: "A political party which openly condemns the idea of economic planning under the pretext of safeguarding freedom is thinking solely in terms of the freedom enjoyed by large corporate employers and by financiers; this kind of freedom, in the present state of affairs, is the very negation of the right of small wage-earners and of the poor to enjoy a just reward for their work, job security, health, etc."[2]

Marchand was obviously expecting government planning to bring financial and occupational security to his union's membership. He was confident that new legislation on freedom of association would favour the expansion of the labour movement. This was at the very moment when he was negotiating with the Lesage government an agreement that included the revision of the province's Labour Code and the unionization of the public service. Marchand hoped that the labour movement might become part of the consultative planning mechanisms and would therefore be able to influence planning considerably. Understandably, he was disturbed by the campaign the Créditistes were waging against the very idea of economic planning.

However, the anxiety displayed by Jean Marchand was not due solely to the fact that the rise of Social Credit was endangering some of the goals pursued by the labour movement. The campaign waged by Réal Caouette was threatening the movement itself and the role which it claimed as exclusive spokesman for the workers of the province. The CNTU's affiliates in the Lake St. John area happened to be heavily con-

2. Ibid.

taminated by Social Credit and it was their members who were swelling the ranks of this right-wing protest movement. The ideological control which the union leadership wanted to maintain over the rank and file was dangerously affected by this development whereby workers sought the answer to their social and economic problems in politics rather than in union solidarity.

During the long hard years of anti-Duplessis resistance, when the main opposition to the government was located outside parliamentary institutions, the leadership of the CNTU earned the loyalty of its members and managed to exercise a jealously guarded ideological control over them. This type of behaviour, which closely resembled that of the Catholic clergy, is characteristic of numerous organizations in Quebec whose roots strike deeply among the people. In this respect, Social Credit had all the appearance of a potential rival that might be able to subvert the loyalty of the union membership and thus destroy the internal strength of the labour movement.

What the leadership of the CNTU found most disconcerting about the Créditiste invasion was the fundamentally anti-intellectual stand in its world view as well as in the negative comments it persistently made about the leaders of other political parties, the labour movement, and the public service. A large number of people at the head of the CNTU were university graduates who felt personally under attack because of their class origins. Specifically, they feared that the Créditistes would exploit class and educational differences between themselves and the rank and file. There was a distinct possibility that class sentiment among union members would cause them to join the Créditistes and reject the intellectuals who dominated the leadership of the CNTU.

This was the first time in the history of Quebec that a ground swell originating from the people was jeopardizing the hold which educated classes maintained over the bulk of the population. It was the first time that a popular movement was self-propelled, as it were, without the inspiration, the support, and the leadership of educated people. It was impossible to do away with the disquieting impression that the Créditiste revolt was directed at university graduates, at professionals, and at the traditional political elite. All the talk directed against the sharks of high finance, the old parties, and other Créditiste targets seemed to be part of some awkward attempt to define the objectives of the political crusade which Caouette was leading. This was the significance that a growing number of people were attributing to this popular upheaval. Given the somewhat paternalistic relationship which the CNTU maintained with industrial workers, its leadership was in a better position than anyone else to understand this.

In French Quebec, class divisions are very different from those in the rest of Canada and in the United States. Social standing is determined by education rather than by wealth. This is due mostly to the historical disabilities from which the French have suffered in connection with economic development and entrepreneurship. There are very few French-speaking people at the top of large national corporations. French savings are usually invested to produce interest and dividends; they are seldom invested in new and speculative ventures. The preeminence of educated people in Quebec stems mostly from their professional activities rather than from their economic power. Admittedly, this situation has been changing rapidly with the development of state capitalism and the slow conversion of Quebec's business life from English to French. At that time, in the early 1960s, the educated classes believed themselves beyond the reach of political protest; they thought themselves untouchable because of the social control they exercised, a kind of control which seemed to be due more to services rendered than to exploitation or domination. But there was nothing they could do to escape the Créditiste challenge, for which there was absolutely no precedent.

The revolt took hold among those elements in the population who were most resentful of the often misguided paternalism of educated elites. Créditiste voters were to be found among those groups who were chronically underrepresented politically and whose needs were most often ignored by authorities.

Working-class areas in Quebec City and in towns throughout the province were extraordinarily receptive to the ideas of Social Credit. They had been very badly served by the previous provincial government, that of the Union Nationale, which was basically hostile to the kind of values associated with industrial labour and urban life. The unions which working-class people joined faced repression on the part of authorities fearful of the tensions which their demands generated in society. During the days of the Union Nationale, the labour movement was a dynamic element favourable to change in the midst of a society dedicated to the preservation of rural traditions and ideals.

The same voters did not see private enterprise in a more favourable light than they saw the government. They were well aware that both of them were in league to preserve an archaic society that had only cheap labour to offer. In addition, big business had a reputation for hostility to the French language because of the exclusivity of its managers and directors. These views were shared by a large number of small wage-earners, tradesmen, clerks, petty functionaries, and impoverished farmers whose economic security had been undermined by low wages and incomes, or by unemployment, and whose occupational horizons were limited by corporate discrimination against the use of French.

The architects of the Quiet Revolution did not enjoy a better reputation. In the countryside as well as in numerous towns across the province, educational reform had the appearance of an ideological war against the past, particularly those aspects which stood in the way of the government's objectives. The determination with which provincial authorities pursued the modernization of mentalities and attitudes heightened the conflict of generations which inevitably surfaces whenever social change is accelerated. Legislation making school attendance compulsory, together with the inordinately long bus rides to which school children were subjected in order to reach the new regional high schools, deprived family farms of vital and inexpensive labour without any kind of compensation. However, the most cutting aspect of the Quiet Revolution was that it seemed to benefit the educated middle class more than the bulk of the population, who hardly had access to the prosperity engendered by the heavy spending of the Lesage government.

Although these grievances originated provincially, they first found expression on the federal scene. This may be explained by the fact that the only party then capable of channelling popular discontent was a federal one. But one must also consider the strange duality exhibited by Quebec society, where public opinion tends to polarize around two centres of government, Ottawa and Quebec, a situation which contributed enormously to perpetuating intergovernmental rivalries.

Réal Caouette's decision to enter the federal scene was very astute from a psychological point of view. What his supporters wanted above all were reforms that would stimulate the economy and produce stable employment and a higher purchasing power. Their expectations were expressed in individual terms rather than in collective ones. In other words they wanted governments to provide solutions for their personal problems and to favour their personal advancement. They rejected the strict controls which they associated with provincial institutions. They could see, if only in a confused manner, that the promotion of personal interests and of individual freedom was somehow related to the exercise of federal power and that provincial power was naturally identified with collective goals and with the subordination of the individual.

Traditional elites were completely taken by surprise at the independence of mind and the individualism displayed at that time by a growing number of workers, tradesmen, and craftsmen in many parts of the province. Nobody had ever thought it would be possible for the people to organize themselves solely through their own efforts and to seek the realization of autonomous political aims. When this in fact did happen, it was immediately perceived as a threat to the hierarchical structure of Quebec society, which more often than not is reflected in official paternalism. Educated classes found it easy to accept the North American standard of living and consumption patterns; more difficult was the populism that had been extremely influential in the U.S. during the latter part of the nineteenth century.

The educated middle class could hardly accept the idea that other social classes might shake off the paternalistic control it had long maintained over them. As the prime beneficiary of the Quiet Revolution, it was eager to expand its economic territory at the expense of the Anglo-Protestant establishment in Montreal. But, given its own economic weakness, the only way the middle class could assert itself was by making use of the historical cohesiveness of the French population. Therefore, it felt profoundly threatened by the anarchic individualism which certain elements were displaying and by the opposition shown to the current economic rationality.

It is tempting to look upon the Créditiste movement as a political aberration, or as a ludicrous episode which for a moment disturbed the natural evolution of Quebec. Yet in no way can it be considered a marginal phenomenon. The movement emerged in the course of an exceptionally tense period of transition from one type of society to a radically different one. Its arrival on the scene coincided with a series of events heralding an extraordinarily profound social mutation.

Among these events the most important was without any doubt the very rapid drop in the birth rate which began to take place after 1957. The rate that year was 29.7 per thousand and it had fallen to 16.3 by 1968.[3] A change of this magnitude is practically unknown in industrialized countries. It shows an accelerated transformation of personal relationships and of popular attitudes towards children and family. It foreshadows new consumption patterns and a somewhat personal and selfish use of available leisure time. In the end, it is a sign of change in social attitudes and personal expectations as well as a relaxation of traditional family bonds. What happened in Quebec, then, was an abrupt and almost brutal break with the

3. *Annuaire du Québec*, 1970 (Québec: Gouvernement du Québec, Ministère de l'Industrie et du Commerce), p. 190.

past affecting all social classes and paving the way for the massive transformations which the Quiet Revolution would later bring about.

As this social upheaval was taking place, the Créditistes were probably the first outside Montreal and the larger industrial towns to reflect the new urban values which the declining birth rate was pointing to. However, it was the marginal character of the Créditistes voters and the general indifference meeting their problems which caused them to become political innovators in Quebec.

The Créditistes made their appearance at the very moment when the Church was resigning itself to a sweeping wave of secularization. Their individualism, their refusal to subordinate personal ambitions to collective interest, emerged just as the separation of Church and state was being put into effect and as Catholicism ceased to be a sort of state religion. Catholicism was no longer a manifestation of civic-mindedness and slowly acquired a more private significance, not unlike Protestantism. The Créditistes did not regret the collapse of the old rural society with its stifling religious presence. Because they were found among the very people whom that society had marginalized, they yearned in their own way for the modernization of Quebec.

The decline of the birth rate and the abdication of the clergy were trends on which the Créditistes had no influence at all. But the rise of nationalism was something else altogether. As feelings of group identity were coming to the fore and as the first terrorist incidents signaled a deterioration of the political climate, Réal Caouette was already active on a number of issues with a strong nationalist flavour. During the election campaigns of 1963, he was often introduced to Créditiste rallies as "le sauveur de la race canadienne-française" (the saviour of the French-Canadian race). This antiquated vocabulary unfortunately distracted attention from the real role which his party was playing in Quebec's social transformation.

The nationalism of Réal Caouette was closely related to that which Henri Bourassa had preached at the beginning of the century: a pan-Canadian vision according to which relations between English and French would be based on equality and mutual respect. However, Caouette was very much aware of the tremendous gap which existed between that ideal and the reality. He did not hesitate, therefore, to deal with ethnic and linguistic questions while politicians on the provincial scene were concerned mostly with constitutional issues.

In the House of Commons and during the election campaign of 1963, Caouette and his principal colleagues spent considerable time discussing the causes of unemployment in Quebec. Beyond the usual economic explanations, they pointed to the fact that French-Canadians were systematically discriminated against in private enterprise as well as in the federal service. Accordingly they persistently called for public-service reform that would provide equal treatment for French and English. The views expressed by the Créditistes ultimately had considerable impact in shops and factories. They paved the way for subsequent union demands for the francization of the workplace, of collective bargaining, and of industrial relations in general.

Growing sensitivity to language issues, however, had little to do with the kind of nationalism that later caused public opinion in Quebec to demand increasingly restrictive legislation on the use of English. Créditiste attitudes had their roots in a desire for personal advancement. The movement was never inclined to rely on government intervention for problems of this nature. Except for the magical management of credit, the role of the state was supposed to be minimal.

The election results of 1962 and 1963 constitute the high-water mark of Social Credit in Quebec. Réal Caouette was never able to repeat these early successes. His party gradually lost the drive that had enabled it to become an effective spokesman for those groups who traditionally had been under-represented in Quebec politics and who still were to a very large degree. Créditiste members of Parliament survived from election to election in the futile hope that a minority government would provide them with the balance of power and with an influence that their numbers could not otherwise justify. Moreover, the very abuses that had favoured the rise of Social Credit were slowly being curtailed. The poorest and most demoralized elements of the population benefited from a reform of the laws governing social aid, small loans, and consumer credit. Educational campaigns on family budgeting launched by the labour movement helped thousands of people to escape from the vicious circle of indebtedness and poverty, and to become productive and responsible citizens once more.

The decisive factor pushing the Créditiste movement into irrelevance was the ideological shift experienced by Quebec voters away from the liberalism which had been characteristic of the first few years of the Quiet Revolution. Imperceptibly, voters turned their backs on a conception of society whereby its strength and dynamism came from the achievements of the individuals that were part of it. They apparently were no longer disposed to believe what the Liberal opposition had preached under the Duplessis regime, that institutions must serve the individual rather than expect loyalty and subservience from him.

The new orthodoxy was in fact just a reprint of the old one. It asserted that the reality of French Quebec was derived from its social, economic, and political institutions which in the end assigned roles to people. This is exactly what the Church and the old rural society had put into practice. With the emergence of the welfare state and of the masses in its charge, Quebec inevitably returned to its former conception of social organization and of the relationship between the individual and society. Political tensions resulting from competition between the two bureaucratic empires in Ottawa and Quebec did the rest: public opinion was diverted from its new-found concern with individualism and personal initiative.

This meant that the educated class of intellectuals and professionals was able to reassert its influence over the people. The social controls which for a moment had been threatened by the impact of the Créditiste movement and of populism were reestablished. Everything was orderly once more, but this was to be for fifteen or twenty years at the most. The rise of the Créditiste movement was a forerunner of profound transformation in the relations between the educated classes of French Canada and the general population, relations which for more than a hundred years have played a determining role in the history of French Quebec.

The Roots of Nationalism

Throughout the twentieth century, the idea of equality has been at the centre of Quebec's preoccupations and it has given a special colouring to contemporary nationalism. It provided the foundation for the claims put forward early in the century by Henri Bourassa in the House of Commons and in the columns of the newspaper *Le Devoir* which he founded in 1910. Later, in 1965, Opposition Leader (later Premier) Daniel Johnson stated the alternative of *Egalité ou indépendance* (equality or independence) as the basis for constitutional negotiations with federal authorities. More recently, when Premier René Lévesque proposed the concept of sovereignty-association, the political independence on which it was expected to rest anticipated that future relations between English and French would be *d'égal à égal* (between equals).

The equality that the vast majority of French-speaking people have in mind is a collective equality, that of individuals being theoretically ensured by the law. This notion has always been a stumbling block to ethnic and cultural coexistence. It has remained incomprehensible for English-speaking people, who as a rule do not think in terms of collectivities and for whom equality is something applicable only to individuals. It stands in contradiction to their idea that the political and economic weight of any community is derived from the sum of its members, of their qualities and their capacity for work. On the French side, however, the commonly shared view is that a community has a life which transcends that of its members.

In the same manner, the meaning given to the word "democracy" is not the same in one language and the other. In

French Quebec, the word is usually taken in the European sense of egalitarian society, of an absence of social and economic divisions. In English Canada, as in the United States, "democracy" refers primarily to electoral processes and to representative institutions. The prevailing concept of democracy scarcely extends beyond the notion of individual rights.

In any case, if Quebec society is so overwhelmingly preoccupied with equality, it is not simply because the concept provides an eloquent way of stating its grievances. Its internal organization and its functioning are in fact egalitarian in spirit. This is what sustains the cohesiveness which French society has consistently displayed throughout its history in Quebec. This egalitarian spirit is to be found nowhere else in North America; Quebec is unique in this respect.

Many visitors to Canada during the eighteenth century pointed this out. In a description of his travels to North America, published in Paris in 1744, Father F.-X. Charlevoix took note of the social equality and the relative absence of economic differentiation in New France, in contrast to the competitive spirit that prevailed in New England. Peter Kalm, a Swedish botanist who visited North America in 1749, made similar observations.

The marked inclination towards egalitarianism stems from a multiplicity of influences. One of them has to do with the seigneurial system which was instituted at the very beginning of the colony and survived until 1854. It was a form of land tenure designed to facilitate settlement and inspired by feudalism. Property rights were held jointly by the seigneur and the *censitaire* who in return for certain community services paid a yearly rent. Until the middle of the nineteenth century, Lower Canada did not have a system of law specifically adapted to commerce or any land registry offices that might stimulate mortgage financing and development. French Quebec was basically a precapitalist society within which the accumulation of capital was seriously inhibited and where the maintenance of equality was perceived as a vital political goal.

While Montreal's English merchants were noisily pressing for the abolition of the seigneurial system because it defied conventional economic thought, the French elites were desperately defending it lest a capitalist invasion rob their community of its ownership of the land. With limited financial resources, with no access to official patronage, and with hardly any professional opportunities in the public service, French-speaking people were confined to a limited range of occupations, the most prestigious of which were medicine, law, and the clergy. These professions, based on the idea of service, helped preserve a feeling of equality and solidarity between the elites and the general population. This basic attitude was reinforced by an increasingly bitter confrontation with the government and the English merchants of Montreal, which finally led to the Rebellion of 1837. It brought to the fore a kind of siege mentality which has often been a component of Quebec nationalism.

Lord Durham was the first to dwell at length on the egalitarian sentiments of the French-speaking population. In his report on the causes of the Rebellion of 1837 in Upper and Lower Canada he analysed its origins and the effect it had on the political life of the country. As did several visitors before him, he saw egalitarianism as a distinctive trait of Lower Canada. He believed it played a key role in shaping events during the generation that preceded the Rebellion and he takes it into account in his recommendations to the imperial government, particularly as regards reorganization of the colonial administration.

Durham was struck by the nature of the educational system he found in French Canada. Its most noteworthy aspects were the care given to the training of elites and the democratic composition of the student body. Most students came from relatively poor rural families. Their intellectual aptitudes had attracted the attention of the parents and of the parish priest who singled them out for free tuition and board in some educational establishment. As they graduated, many of them joined the clergy. The others, however, often could not find a suitable occupation producing an adequate income because most of the careers in the public service and in the militia were monopolized by English-speaking people. Hence, the majority among them eventually gravitated towards law and medicine, which they practised in their native villages with varying degrees of success: the population was neither numerous nor prosperous enough to support them. Durham believed this situation was at the core of the Canadian problem. He describes it with a vocabulary which betrays considerable antipathy towards the French:

> Thus the persons of most education in every village belong to the same families, and the same original station in life, as the illiterate habitants whom I have described. They are connected with them by all the associations of early youth and the ties of blood. The most perfect equality marks their intercourse, and the superior in education is separated by no barrier of manners, or pride, or distinct interests, from the singularly ignorant peasantry by which he is surrounded. He combines, therefore, the influences of superior knowledge and social equality, and wields a power over the mass, which I do not believe that the educated class of any other portion of the world possess.[1]

Even though the picture drawn by Durham is somewhat antagonistic and almost like a caricature, it is readily apparent that French society was unusually homogeneous and that its very high degree of cohesiveness was related to the leadership of the educated classes. However, the prevailing mood of egalitarianism was not due only to local institutions and habits of mind. As Durham noted, there were also some external causes:

> The most uninstructed population anywhere trusted with political power, is thus placed in the hands of a small body

1. *Lord Durham's Report: An Abridgement of "Report on the Affairs of British North America,"* ed. Gerald M. Craig (Toronto: McClelland and Stewart, Carleton Library, 1963), p. 30.

of instructed persons, in whom it reposes the confidence which nothing but such domestic connexion, and such community of interest could generate. Over the class of persons by whom the peasantry are thus led, the government has not acquired, or even laboured to acquire, influence; its members have been thrown into opposition by the system of exclusion, long prevalent in the colony; and it is by their agency that the leaders of the Assembly have been enabled hitherto to move as one mass, in whatever direction they thought proper, the simple and ductile population of the country.[2]

According to Lord Durham, if the colonial government had taken the trouble to extend the benefits of education to the population as a whole, it might have prevented the rise of the elitist mentality which gave the French such great political force. The government would not have found itself under the obligation of crushing the power of those it called the Demagogues and whose best-known leader was Louis-Joseph Papineau. This is the situation which resulted in the country being ungovernable and becoming prey to agitators against existing laws and against public order.

The political institutions of that period contributed enormously to the chain of events leading to rebellion and civil strife. As did all other British colonies in North America, Lower Canada had a representative Assembly enabled to vote laws and outlays of public funds. However, executive authority was vested in the hands of the British governor and his council. Responsible government, as we know it today, did not exist at the time. The Parti Patriote, which was the first political expression of French nationalism, was able to advance the most daring proposals knowing full well that it would never find itself under the obligation of putting them into effect. The prospects of exercising power, which can bring a certain degree of realism to political debates, did not exist. Because of that, the colony inevitably drifted into paralysing

2. Ibid.

confrontations between the governor, the executive council, and the English merchants of Montreal on one side, and the Assembly led by French intellectuals and professionals on the other.

It was during the early part of the nineteenth century that militant nationalism first appeared among the population. Of course, patriotic sentiment and the idea of forming a distinct nationality had existed long before and had been expressed on countless occasions. However, during the period which preceded the Rebellion of 1837, nationalism came to dominate political processes and it took the form of relentless opposition to the British governors and to the English-speaking merchants of Montreal. The mobilization of a substantial proportion of the population in the cause of nationalism characterized this difficult period, which was affected by adverse economic conditions and a sharp decline in agricultural productivity.

The rise of nationalism coincided with that of a new class of educated professionals who assumed political leadership in the towns and in the countryside and who eventually came to dominate the Assembly. It displaced the older class of seigneurs and even managed to undermine seriously the influence of the Catholic clergy on the political and social views of the population. Indeed, as a result of the dramatic intensity with which it approached every public issue, the new bourgeoisie was successful in imposing its own conception of the way French society in Lower Canada should evolve. The basic attitudes and behaviour which it displayed at that time have proved to be so durable that they can still be detected among contemporary nationalist elements.

Conditions in Lower Canada at the beginning of the nineteenth century offered fertile ground for nationalist agitation. However, the newly educated class of doctors, lawyers, and notaries hardly needed an outside stimulus: it had its own internal reasons for formulating a world view centred on national solidarity. The status of its members, their relationship with the general population, the very limitations of their social functions, everything pushed this particular class to place the concept of nationality at the very centre of its mental universe and to give it greater importance than any other factor.

The most obvious consideration is that this new class remained a virtual prisoner of its original environment. The intellectual vision to which its members had acceded through education failed to open on wider social horizons than those that had been available before. Upward mobility was blocked and in any event offered very little except prestige and a certain material well-being related to the exercise of law or medicine. Professionals were dependent on an exclusively local practice and on people whose means were severely limited by general economic conditions. Bonds of friendship and of kinship kept them among a poorly educated if not actually illiterate population.

The social environment was so lacking in diversity that professional life was confined to the most elementary activities. Cities such as Montreal and Quebec offered few opportunities to enterprising persons because of the monopoly which the English merchant class maintained of careers in commerce and public administration. There were few prospects for advancement and self-renewal, with the result that the larger part of the French-speaking elite was confined to a narrowly circumscribed world affording little intellectual gratification. The lack of a well-informed and interested public severely curtailed literary and cultural activities.

Politics was the only domain where lawyers, notaries, and doctors could engage in stimulating and rewarding activities; moreover, it seemed to offer a possibility of resuming an interrupted social ascent. However, because of the circumstances and the characteristics of the society in which they happened to be living, the educated professional class approached public affairs in a very particular frame of mind, one which compelled them to challenge existing political institutions. Because they were practically confined to their native communities and because the possibilities of upward mobility were denied them, people in the liberal professions set out to overcome everything that seemed to be in opposition to the collective will. Obviously, they themselves would assume the task of defining its contents and its objectives as well as providing the political leadership necessary to achieve them.

Social groups finding themselves in this type of situation tend to direct their resentment and frustration against the dominant power. Because of the many external constraints weighing upon them, they usually adopt a pessimistic view of their own future and at the same time they are prone to formulate collective projects which are markedly utopian in spirit. These groups sustain their self-esteem by glorifying tradition and the historical past. They put forward ideological systems which maximize their own role in society and they press for the kind of change that will make them into the new dominant power. It was this model which the educated class of lawyers, notaries, and doctors followed during the decisive period at the beginning of the nineteenth century and expressed through their political arm, the Parti Patriote.

The new class, as a result of its exclusion from the economic system and its profits, gradually came to reject the values and the rationality associated with the commercial capitalism of that period. The most striking element in its political involvement was a determination to take every opportunity of thwarting it, particularly as regards the introduction of commercial law which English merchants desperately wanted as an antidote to the stagnation prevailing in the colony. But the French took up the defence of the seigneurial regime which, because of its system of land tenure inspired from feudalism, presented a legal armour which English capitalism could not breach. This closed and idealized system accurately reflected a widely expressed desire for national isolation. Later, at the time of the Rebellion and just when overpopulation and excessive subdivision of land had brought the seigneurial system to the verge of collapse, many people were dreaming of a sort of agrarian capitalism inspired by the American Revolution which had taken place some three generations earlier.

The seigneurial system consistently displayed a strong propensity towards utopianism. It sought to strengthen political defences against the inroads of mercantile capitalism, whose principal impact was to heighten the colony's economic dependence on outside markets and prevent the growth of an autonomous and self-reliant society. This type of capitalism, which relied on highly speculative investments in resources, introduced economic individualism into a society where egalitarianism was the dominant ideology and where diversity and differentiation resided primarily in the social roles which individuals chose or were forced to assume.

The rise of the liberal professions in the early part of the nineteenth century and the exercise of political influence through the Parti Patriote constitute one of the most important turning points in the evolution of French society in Canada. During this period, there appeared tensions which, in spite of the negative and destructive attitudes leading to the 1837 Rebellion, were instrumental in shaping collective consciousness.

This new class of professionals soon clashed with the Catholic clergy which, although opposed to the capitalism of the English merchants, hoped that expressions of loyalty to imperial authorities would help temper its worst effects. Papineau and the Patriotes refused to see things in this light. For a long time they had stopped believing in the role of arbitrator which the imperial government had been expected to play in the affairs of Lower Canada. On the contrary, the imperial government was perceived as a party to the persecution and repression which weighed down the French-Canadian nation. The Patriotes became the leading spokesmen for the will to resist, and they eventually bridged the gap separating verbal from physical violence.

Tensions between the class of professionals and the clergy resulted from vigorous efforts to monopolize the social and ideological allegiance of the population. The Patriotes, who dominated the Assembly, were sometimes openly anticlerical and on several occasions they attempted to put an end to the historical compact between Church and state. This was an agreement which gave Anglo-Protestants complete freedom to administer their community affairs as well as to organize the economic life of the colony as they saw fit.

The failure of the Rebellion as well as the repression to which it gave rise contributed to a serious decline in the influence wielded by the professional elite. The legislative union of Upper and Lower Canada placed the French population at the mercy of an English majority. This development, which took place in 1840, completely altered the rules of the game in the sphere of politics. The former struggles for the preservation of the seigneurial system and its replacement with some kind of agrarian republic had suddenly lost all their relevance.

Henceforth, political activity concentrated on two main objectives. The first was to ensure the survival of the French-Canadian nation within the new political institutions. The second was to end the economic stagnation which was slowly throttling the colony. The most obvious solution was to come to terms with the new industrial capitalism which in the United States and in England had already displaced the old commercial order. In the context of the period, success required an approach to politics radically different from that which had prevailed during the first part of the nineteenth century.

Stubborn resistance and confrontation necessarily gave way to cooperation and bargaining. The new situation called for a new type of political involvement and for a view of society diametrically opposed to the resentment that had inspired the troubled period leading to the Rebellion. Instead of magnifying each grievance out of all proportion and unconditionally calling for a favourable settlement, the generation of politicians who made their appearance after 1840 began to act with a very acute sense of the real weight of the various ethnic, social, and economic groups that had been brought together. The aggressive and uncompromising demeanour which had been the foundation of Papineau's reputation was completely out of style in the period after 1837. His successors began to act as intermediaries and political brokers between the authorities and the people. The prototype of this new kind of politician was Louis-Hippolyte Lafontaine, a former Patriote and Papineau supporter.

The shock resulting from the failure of the Rebellion had brought about, within less than a generation, a complete transformation of mentalities. Order, tolerance, and conformity became the rule, facilitating a fruitful alliance with reformist elements in Upper Canada. The latter were eager to put an end to the favouritism and the abuses of power associated with the British governors and the economic interests they were identified with.

Accordingly, French Canada ceased perceiving itself in terms of a homogeneous and undifferentiated group. It became necessary to accept the fact that society would henceforth show an unprecedented variety of interests and attitudes, something for which population growth and economic expansion were largely responsible. The new pluralism was accompanied by a rather positive attitude towards industrial investment and progress. Instead of idealizing the past or seeing the future with either apprehension or utopian longings, there was a resurgence of confidence in individual capacity for action and in the benefits to be derived from a greater display of energy and initiative. Underlying sentiments of collective solidarity gradually adapted themselves to the individualism which had already started to dissolve French Canada's historical egalitarianism.

This transformation occurred in opposition to the nationalist ideology which had concentrated within itself all the social and economic preoccupations of a period that was then receding into the past. The political influence wielded by members of the liberal professions was slowly eroded. When Louis-Joseph Papineau managed to get himself elected to the Parliament of the United Provinces on his return from exile in 1845, he was forced to acknowledge that his ability to shape events was infinitely smaller than the general esteem in which he was then held. His time had passed.

For a period of about twenty-five years, a greater diversity and breadth of economic interests produced a new ideological pluralism. No particular class or group was able to exert the kind of leadership and control which had been characteristic of the period before the Rebellion. Given the minority situation of the French population, national sentiment was bound to survive. But nationalism itself no longer constituted the basis for political action and the rallying point of collective interests.

It is not surprising therefore that religious sentiment should have been on the rise during this whole period. Problems of social organization and of economic survival receded into the background as the population recovered from the agricultural crisis that had brought about the collapse and the abolition of the seigneurial system and as the economic outlook became more positive. French-Canadians therefore satisfied their desire for unity and solidarity through the practice of religion. This desire had been monopolized for a long time by political action but could no longer be satisfied in that way under the new Union government of 1840. The faith and the religious fervour which emerged then, however, were very different from those that would appear after 1860, at about the time of Confederation.

Adaptation to industrial capitalism as proposed by Lafontaine was essentially a pragmatic response which needed to be sustained by some ideology that was not in direct competition with it and whose main area of concern lay outside politics and economics. This is what religion represented at that time. But it was not a totally institutionalized faith whose mission was to provide leadership and control for an impoverished and isolated society. It was a personal kind of faith, one that met personal problems at a time when collective action offered few encouraging prospects.

In any case, religion satisfied a craving for ideals as no other activity could. The Patriotes, for a certain period of time when they were challenging the established order, were able to become the intellectual mentors of the population and to introduce new ideas of democracy and political freedom. But once stimulating tensions had disappeared, this relatively small elite and the bulk of the population that followed it were no longer able to pursue their intellectual quest in the field of politics. It was religion that took over.

Such a change was inescapable. The cultural and social gap which separated Canada from France was becoming wider year by year. When nationalism first appeared in Lower Canada — around 1810, supposing a date can be put on it — the colony had been British for a little less than fifty years. Books and ideas from France retained their relevance for quite some time in spite of the social upheaval associated with the French Revolution and the Napoleonic era. But after 1840 attitudes had become too divergent for French intellectual activity to exert any meaningful influence on the French population of Canada, except for a few educated and privileged groups. The only literature imported from France that remained within the comprehension of the average reader was religious and pedagogical, and this is what provided the foundation of the book trade during that period. In 1855 an inventory of volumes stocked in the bookstore owned and operated by Edouard-Raymond Fabre, former Patriote and mayor of Montreal, showed them to be 53 per cent religious and 34 per cent pedagogical.[3]

In spite of the short-lived pessimism which took hold in the aftermath of the Rebellion's defeat, and although national sentiment was subordinated to practical problems of industrial expansion and economic growth, this period gave rise to considerable cultural activity. The foundation of Laval University in 1852 and the establishment of a network of elementary schools helped broaden personal horizons and improve the general quality of life. The immigration of several religious orders from France at the same time provided the educated manpower necessary to sustain this cultural renaissance and, incidentally, to consolidate the growing interest in religion.

Little by little, the clergy assumed control of all cultural and social institutions in Lower Canada, and set out to impose rigid and austere moral standards in its pronouncements on

3. Jean-Louis Roy, *Edouard-Raymond Fabre, libraire et patriote canadien (1799–1854)* (Montréal: Hurtubise HMH, 1974), p. 71.

literature, politics, and society in general. It also launched a sustained attack on the predominant liberal thought of that period, which had been shaped earlier by the Patriotes and which was then influenced by contemporary French writers such as Victor Hugo and Lamennais. The Institut canadien in Montreal, which was at the centre of the reformist and liberal movement, found itself increasingly isolated as the attacks of the Church and clergy gathered momentum. It finally closed in 1865.

The event which confirmed the hegemony of the Church, and the triumph of the values with which it was identified, was Confederation in 1867. The new constitutional order replacing the legislative union of Upper and Lower Canada was greeted with satisfaction and optimism by most people, in spite of the deep-seated distrust shown by some members of the parliamentary opposition. Confederation solved the problem of the Union government, whose finances were becoming chaotic and whose freedom of action came to be paralysed by ministerial instability. It unified the British provinces of North America as a prelude to a westward push for settlement and trade. Finally, Confederation brought a practical solution to the thorny problem of integrating a French-speaking population into a political system which had fallen completely under the power of an English majority.

For French Canadians, Confederation was not simply a union; in a direct and immediate way, it seemed to be an actual separation. The theme of a new nationality as interpreted by McGee, Brown, Macdonald and even Cartier, hardly stirred Lower Canada, contrary to what was happening in Upper Canada and in the Maritimes. There, ethnic and linguistic solidarity fostered the hope that Confederation would give birth to a new nationality similar to that of the motherland. But this was not the dream of Lower Canada where the principal mission of the new provincial government was believed to be the preservation of the characteristics of the French-Canadian nation. Indeed, according to *La Minerve* [a leading newspaper], "such is the significance that must be attached to this new constitution. One may interpret it as the recognition of French-Canadian nationality. As a distinct and separate nationality we constitute a state within a state, with the full enjoyment of our rights and the formal recognition of our national independence."[4]

It is within the framework of this provincial state, endowed with a circumscribed but no less real sovereignty, that the Catholic clergy imposed its world view and its ideas for the future of the French-Canadian nation. The very existence of such a state, which represented a majority of French-speaking people, made it possible for the Church to extend its influence considerably, something that would have been impossible under the Union government or under any other constitution. By pressing on individual consciences, the clergy was able to exert a determining influence on the policies of the new provincial administration. It managed to acquire, through a delegation of authority, complete control over some of its constitutional responsibilities, particularly in the organization of community activities and services.

The anticlericalism and the liberalism of previous periods had no permanent effect on the prestige of the Church among the general population. Its internal organization, its democratic methods of recruitment, and, most of all, its historical antecedents in Lower Canada, served to inspire the utmost confidence. This helps to explain the surprising ease with which the Church rallied the majority to its point of view and forced the minority into ideological submission. The clergy displaced the professional middle class and assumed the task of determining the political orientation and the collective goals of the French-speaking population.

The Church in Lower Canada, contrary to the situation then prevailing in other Catholic countries in Western

4. Marcel Hamelin, *Les premières années du parlementarisme québécois* *(1867–1878)* (Québec: Les Presses de l'Université Laval, 1974), pp. 7–8.

Europe, had the great advantage of not being divided into a high and a low clergy and of not being associated with a decadent economic caste. Very close to the people, its leaders had come to realize that their influence and their authority could be maintained and enlarged to the extent that they obtained the support of the people....

The prestige and authority of the Catholic Church in Lower Canada—a situation which has prevailed until the present day—was due to the fact that it always benefited simultaneously from the privileges of aristocratic continuity and of the advantages of democratic recruitment. Its leaders and its members possessed in common an administrative experience, or a psychological capital, which was being transmitted from generation to generation and continuously enriched.[5]

From the very beginning of the colony, the Church was the sole institution affording the people an opportunity to participate in some form of public administration. The only available experience of popular and democratic participation was the election of churchwardens, who publicly discussed the best way to spend tithes for the construction and maintenance of churches and presbyteries. This democratic exercise, though limited in scope, helped perpetuate the close bonds which had long existed between the Church and the people.

Until the middle of the nineteenth century, implementation of expenditures and laws voted by the Assembly came under the authority of the British governor and of a council chosen by himself. It was only after eight years of tense political struggle that the Parliament of the United Provinces, created in 1840, managed to obtain recognition for the principle of ministerial responsibility and of the subordination of executive authority to an elected assembly. At about the same time, the United Provinces created the first elected councils for the administration of municipalities and school boards. Until then,

5. Michel Brunet, *Notre passé, le présent et nous* (Montréal: Fides, 1976), pp. 72, 78.

only the councils set up to administer certain Church properties combined the democratic principles of representativeness, participation, and responsibility.

It is not surprising, therefore, that the Church should have been able to impose the parish as the basic social unit in French Canada and promote an ideological system which enhanced its own role, and that it should persistently have tried to undermine the role of the provincial state which, within the federal system, could have grown into a dangerous rival.

Within this society, which for all practical purposes was confined to Quebec, the clergy soon became the dominant and most active elite. Its political beliefs readily rallied most elements within the population. Quebec then evolved into a closed system founded upon agriculture and rural life and which, like the seigneurial system in the first part of the nineteenth century, happened to be in striking contrast with the rest of North America. The Catholic clergy strove to preserve the basic principles of social utility and equality which from the very beginning profoundly influenced popular attitudes.

Just as the Patriotes had fought commercial capitalism, the clergy stood against the industrial capitalism of the second half of the nineteenth century. The organization of industrial production and the urban life to which it was linked were seen as a direct threat to the kind of social cohesion on which the Church's influence was based. This cohesion rested on innumerable family and community bonds and was upheld by the large number of services which had the parish as a focal point; these provided a type of control from which it was practically impossible to escape.

However, the clergy and the Church did not dare launch a frontal assault against capitalism. The confrontation would have been hopeless because of the political structures of the country, which imposed severe limitations on the sovereignty of the provincial government and gave federal authorities prime responsibility for the economic well-being of the whole country. Accordingly, the clergy resigned itself to the promotion of rural life, leaving aside the increasingly pressing problems of industrialization and urbanization. There was a passive reliance on what was usually referred to as the social doctrine of the Church, as expounded in Rome.

In spite of an intellectual discourse which to all appearances was at variance with that of the Patriotes and of the professional middle class, the clergy clung to some very similar attitudes. Just as its lay predecessors had done before, the new religious elite saw the nation's salvation in isolation and marginalization with respect to the dominant Anglo-Protestant culture of North America. Its economic thinking was limited to denying the values associated with the organization of industrial activity and to asserting the primacy of the intellectual, social, and spiritual values with which French-speaking elites had been closely identified in Quebec.

It was all the easier to pursue this policy in that English Canada also continued to depend on the same thought processes that had been at the root of the earlier confrontations. The subordination of social and cultural values to economic interests left little room for fruitful cooperation between English and French communities in Canada.

The common incapacity or refusal to integrate social and economic values in a coherent world view inevitably produced in Canada two truncated societies subject to periodic political seizures.

Artists and Nationalism

There are privileged areas which, in the minds of most people, are beyond the contingencies of everyday life. Sports is one of them, and so is whatever pertains to the pursuit of aesthetic goals. It is always with a great deal of resentment that athletes and spectators, or artists and audiences, see the intrusion of politics in these two areas. Those who are engaged in a dramatization of human experience will inevitably seek to protect the integrity of their respective domains against the subversion that results from political intervention. All these sporting or artistic activities seem to be endowed with an almost sacred character, one might say, which transcends everyday life, and any intrusion from the prosaic world of politics will consequently be rejected as a sort of sacrilege.

However, there are mixed and even contradictory attitudes as regards nationalism, which may be described as the politicization of national sentiment or patriotism. Nationalism very frequently makes use of literature: the theatre, the novel, and poetry; it reverts to simple patriotism when it resorts to means of expression that do not rely on words, such as music and painting. Attitudes will diverge widely in the case of classical music whenever it is accompanied by a text linking it to religion or to an ideological cause such as nationalism, marxism, or even feminism.

Obviously, individual reactions will depend on the extent to which each person is willing to subordinate his vision of the world to a concept such as nationalism. Acceptance or rejection will vary according to individuals and according to the significance attributed to various modes of expression. It is also possible to categorize reactions on the basis of the audience and according to the level of seriousness perceived in individual works or in particular genres.

The serious financial problems which threatened the very existence of the Montreal Symphony Orchestra towards the end of 1973 serve to illustrate the role which nationalism and national sentiment may play in public administration and in the resolution of such a crisis in the arts. The problems of the MSO arose at a time when nationalism in Quebec was becoming increasingly demanding and aggressive and when it was being used by those who hoped to provoke accelerated and radical social transformations.

In November 1973 the chairman of the MSO board, Robert J. Bruck, took everyone by surprise when he announced that the orchestra would have to suspend operations in a month's time because of the unmanageable size of its accumulated deficit. About one hundred musicians and fifteen staff employees would have to be laid off. The statement, obviously designed for shock value, sought to persuade authorities in Ottawa and Quebec City that they should be more generous with subsidies for classical music. The provincial minister for cultural affairs, Denis Hardy, replied immediately that there could be no question of allowing an institution such as the Montreal Symphony Orchestra to disband and that some way would be found to take care of the deficit. However, he added that after this rescue operation it would be necessary to assess the quality of the orchestra's management and its role in the cultural life of the city and of the province. The minister also indicated that should the government be called upon to assume the deficit it would insist on delegating a director to the orchestra's board.

The prime minister of Canada, Pierre Elliott Trudeau, had also been approached in a last-ditch attempt to save the orchestra after its request for special funding had been turned down by the Canada Council. The prime minister was the first to draw the public's attention to the real nature of the orchestra's problems, and this he did directly and unsparingly. His views were stated in a letter addressed to Mr. Bruck, the text of which was subsequently released. After having explained that the Montreal Symphony had been the most generously subsidized orchestra in the country, the prime minister then broached the thorny question of intercultural and interethnic relations in Montreal.

Another difficulty, in our estimation, is the apparent lack of sufficiently broad support for the MSO from within the community that it serves. Montreal's English-language citizens have accorded strong, generous, and continued support to the orchestra ever since it was founded, but the MSO has not succeeded in establishing itself as an institution "belonging" to Montreal's French-language community to anywhere the same extent. If I rely on the testimony of those who are competent to make such a judgment, I am led to believe that the impossibility in which the orchestra finds itself of overcoming at least part of its financial difficulties can be attributed to this unfortunate fact.[1]

The prime minister's statement caused a certain amount of uneasiness in Montreal's English-speaking community, which at the time felt deeply threatened by the rapid escalation of nationalist sentiment in Quebec. Most people thought it offensive to claim that the orchestra's problems could be attributed to a supposed lack of consideration shown the French-speaking community. On this occasion, the board chairman stepped in to defend the English community and himself as well:

The MSO has never been a battleground for our language conflicts and it must never be allowed to become one.... The prime minister would be the last person to expect that the crisis of the MSO could be resolved by fanning the flames of conflict between French- and English-speaking citizens.

"Those who suggest that there could be some inequality in the interest shown by the two major linguistic communities of

1. Le Devoir, 7 December 1973 (author's translation).

Montreal... are trying to distort the problem," continued Bruck, who also regretted that "certain persons are trying to make political or personal capital out of a painful crisis whose outcome concerns all Montrealers equally."[2]

Bruck then proceeded to compound his own difficulties. In his view, the problems of the orchestra should not be attributed solely to the board of which he was chairman. They had been coming to a head under previous administrations and they were normal in the growth of a first-rate organization such as Montreal's. The crisis would have been readily overcome, he said, "if we had opted for mediocrity instead of insisting on excellence." He then drove the point home and, as Michel Roy noted in *Le Devoir*, it caused considerable resentment:

> "Certain people are now asking us to broaden our base so as to include more numerous elements in the community. I fully agree with this. It has been our goal for many years. Unfortunately, serious music is not as easily popular as professional hockey..." The contempt, conscious or not, which this statement conveys startled many journalists and critics or made them shudder.[3]

The attitude of the orchestra's board chairman is all the more surprising in that his organization was at the outset almost exclusively French-speaking. It was founded in 1934 under the name of La Société des Concerts Symphoniques de Montréal following the refusal of the Montreal Orchestra to give satisfaction to a body of music lovers who rebelled against the exaggerated importance given English musicians and composers. The latter were having great difficulty in acceding to universal forms of expression and they managed to please only those whose religious and cultural affinities tied them to the British Isles. The French concert-going public in Montreal refused to submit any longer to aesthetic standards

2. *Le Devoir*, 4 December 1973 (author's translation).
3. Ibid.

which it felt to be foreign and entirely inappropriate, both as regards the works played and the artists hired. Hence the appearance of a rival orchestra.

In any event, the Montreal Orchestra was forced to close down in the early 1940s. Because its repertory catered too exclusively to the tastes of the Anglo-Protestant minority, it could not count on the loyalty and continuing support of other groups in the city. The Jewish community, for example, was then becoming more affluent and its cultural interests were broader and more sophisticated. Many Jewish people had a musical culture rooted in Germany and in central Europe and they naturally gravitated towards the Société des Concerts Symphoniques with its more international outlook. Some time later, the French orchestra rallied the support of those members of the Anglo-Protestant community who were closely involved with the management of large Canadian corporations. The supplementary funding that became available allowed the orchestra to expand and gradually raise its standards to the level of the best orchestras in North America.

As the orchestra grew and matured, there were fundamental changes in its character. With the idea of reaching a broader public, management increased the number of concerts and expanded the repertory. It became necessary to hire more musicians in order to perform the great symphonic works of the late nineteenth and early twentieth centuries, a period which represents the high point of orchestral gigantism. New sources of financing were tapped to meet a rapidly expanding budget.

By the middle of the 1950s, the orchestra of the Société des Concerts Symphoniques had little to do with the community spirit which prevailed at the time of its foundation some twenty years earlier. Imperceptibly a new set of goals was substituted for the original ones of satisfying the tastes of a French-speaking public and providing professional opportunities for local artists. The orchestra's French roots came to be overshadowed by management's desire to reflect the universal values associated with the whole repertory of classical music, values which can exert a powerful influence even though they cannot be defined precisely. The orchestra eventually became international or cosmopolitan in its spirit as well as in its composition. The modest goals of its early days were completely set aside.

In the social and economic circumstances prevailing in Montreal at that time, such a transformation inevitably meant that the city's English-speaking community would take charge of the orchestra, thereby bringing about a noticeable decline of French influence over its organization, administration, and artistic direction. As governments were not yet disposed to practise cultural intervention, matters were allowed to take their course. Representatives of large national corporations, who happened to be providing a large part of the funds on which the orchestra depended, came to exert a determining influence on management and slowly imposed their own cultural values.

Musical life in Montreal gradually integrated with that of the North American continent, a trend which the public unquestionably supported. Management began putting into effect the policies and practices which had worked so well for the best American orchestras, such as those of New York, Boston, and Philadelphia, which were seen by French- and English-speaking Montrealers as models to be imitated. Another extremely important factor favouring cultural continentalism was the presence of the Musicians' Guild of Montreal, a union affiliated with the American Federation of Musicians. Collective bargaining and special agreements contributed to creating a continental job market for musicians and to imposing continental standards on the entertainment industry. The Guild helped do away with the parochialism of Montreal, but at the same time contributed to levelling its distinguishing characteristics.

The English language gradually assumed a preeminent place in the internal operations of the orchestra. This situation, just as many others similar to it, shows the great disparity which exists between the two main language groups in the city. The English community draws its strength not only from its control of the economy and its near-monopoly of the leading jobs in industry and commerce. Its affinity with American culture, which happens to be exceptionally active in music, serves to enhance its commanding position. Consequently, it becomes almost impossible for French culture to assert itself in what one might call a situation of free competition. This explains why French elites in Quebec are often tempted to fall back on cultural protectionism and to work towards the isolation of their own society from all outside influences.

It is under such circumstances that nationalism comes to the fore and makes itself felt. It received a great deal of encouragement from the orchestra's board chairman, as a result of his verbal lapses and his inability to understand the political context he was operating in. But in the end there was little Bruck could do but accept responsibility for the limited interest which the orchestra aroused among the French-speaking community of Montreal, as Trudeau had suggested: "For too long the MSO has been influenced by the fact that 90 per cent of the orchestra's revenues came from 10 per cent of the Montreal community, that is, the part made up of large corporations and companies."[4]

The people who were the most aggressive in their denunciations of the Montreal Symphony were left-wing nationalists. They saw it as "the very symbol of cultural colonialism in Quebec." The weekly *Québec-Presse*, in an editorial signed by Robert Lévesque, accused it of having hardly more than twenty French-speaking members out of the ninety-seven permanent musicians it had hired. Other grievances were the use of English as the language of work and Bruck's inability to express himself in French.

> The reprehensible aspect of the MSO's situation is that for several decades it has not belonged to the French community in Montreal, which still happens to be the second largest French city in the world. This *American orchestra in Montreal* has never made any effort to incorporate in its membership, in its management, or in its repertory, anything from Quebec.... What happens is this: music students

4. *Le Devoir*, 12 January 1974 (author's translation).

in Quebec colleges hardly stand a chance of being hired by the MSO. They must either give up or find work abroad. We have an orchestra that is subsidized out of public funds but which will never call upon conductors from Quebec; they too must go abroad.[5]

Three months earlier, before the crisis in the MSO had become public knowledge, the same weekly suggested in the headline to an interview with producer Michel Gélinas: "Give to those who are creating the real Québécois culture the millions that now go to the symphony and the opera." "Perhaps this could be a way of putting a stop to the massive movement of our young people towards Anglo-Saxon music, because those who are composing here do not have the means of meeting foreign competition," said Gélinas, who incidentally was defending himself from the charge of hiring too many artists from France for his shows, at the expense of Quebec talent.

This kind of accusation should be addressed instead to the government and to the various bodies responsible for the arts. It is a shame to see the very great efforts that are wasted just to make us look good.

A million dollars is swallowed up annually by the symphony, a half-million by the Opera and all the other prestige productions. In whose interest? Just catering to the megalomania of a few people, to please the ears of 0.01 per cent of the population. I would go even further than that. I would say that subsidized organizations like the Théâtre du Nouveau Monde and other theatre groups are shamelessly wasting our money. For instance, what is the use of a workshop to make costumes for the TNM, that must be costing thousands of dollars, while they could make do with something less sumptuous. All that money could be given over to grants and bursaries for young artists, for

5. *Québec-Presse*, 9 December 1973 (author's translation).

people who have ideas but no means of putting them into effect.[6]

The Parti Québécois spokesman on cultural affairs in the National Assembly, Claude Charron, suggested that the government put the symphony squarely under trusteeship instead of delegating a director who would simply be acting as a watchdog. This would be the most efficient way of ensuring that its policies meet the real needs of Quebec. "At the present time, the orchestra includes many musicians who are not from Quebec, while students at the Conservatory have no professional outlet on the labour market," he said.

The financial troubles which came to a head in 1973 brought two opposing concepts of classical music to the surface. It confronted the English community and its obsessive fear of nationalism, with an important section of the French community, precisely the one most inclined towards nationalist ideas and most resentful of the penetration of English language and culture. The deep-seated desire of these nationalist elements to preserve the autonomy of French cultural activity in Quebec is what persuaded the federal and provincial governments to intervene directly in the affairs of the MSO and to support one concept of the role of music at the expense of the other.

In the eyes of the English community, at least that part of it which is interested in the arts, the symphony represents one of the many links it wants to preserve with the rest of Canada and with the United States. This organization, like the Montreal Museum of Fine Arts, is expected to be the cultural counterpart of the community's professional and economic horizons, which are felt to include all of North America and beyond. The sentiment of belonging to a worldwide culture, dominant in technology and commerce, exerts a profound influence on social attitudes. One may readily perceive a certain impatience at the inappropriate and untimely demands of the French population, whose tastes and

6. *Québec-Presse*, 23 September 1973 (author's translation).

interests seem to be those of a society closed in on itself and seeking to remain isolated.

The gnawing fear of becoming virtual prisoners of French society in Quebec has a very immediate effect on the attitudes which English-speaking people will collectively display in a variety of circumstances. For instance, there is hardly any trace in Montreal of that Canadian nationalism which periodically comes to the fore in Toronto and in other large cities in Canada. Nor is there any sympathy towards political parties that urge greater public involvement in cultural and economic institutions. It is as if the promotion of local and community interests might endanger the very links that most people want to preserve with the world outside Quebec. Only the very threatening pressures of the French majority will bring out a certain concern with roots and a feeling of collective identity among the English-speaking population of Montreal.

Significantly, no one seems to be interested in any form of protectionism that would sustain local demand for certain types of skills. It would seem absolutely senseless to most English-speaking people in Montreal to demand, as spokesmen for the French community have been doing on its behalf, that the symphony provide a greater number of jobs for graduates of their community's music schools. Everyone expects them to make their way as best they can, to compete with musicians from other parts of North America, and to be prepared to leave town for the sake of their careers. Such an attitude is characteristic of English Montreal and one can see its applications in many areas other than music, for example business and scientific research.

This continentalist attitude runs counter to the policies of the federal government, which is seeking to promote an original Canadian culture, in both English and French, through various agencies such as the Canadian Broadcasting Corporation, the National Film Board, and the Canada Council. But Ottawa's cultural nationalism has had unfortunate side effects on the English community in Montreal by inadvertently encouraging the concentration of English-language production in Toronto, just as Montreal has been made the cultural capital of French Canada. Or, seen from another angle, the life of the arts tends to follow that of the economy and of politics; it seeks to give it expression.

One should not ignore, in this context, the symbolic character of the symphonic music which is the orchestra's mainstay. Its point of greatest development came towards the end of the nineteenth century, just when social organization in the more advanced countries finally adjusted to the requirements of industrial production and when imperialism and colonialism were spreading these new forms of organization throughout the world. While concert halls were growing ever larger, more and more musicians were necessary to fill the newly available sound space. Symphony orchestras necessarily became highly disciplined ensembles responding to conductors whose tyrannical authority enabled them to interpret works that became steadily more ambitious, demanding, and grandiose. As a result of some mysterious subterranean connection, symphony orchestras were reproducing the spirit of large industrial complexes.

There was no lack of composers to take advantage of the means newly placed at their disposal. Most of them glorified the new social order. But the greatest acted as the spokesmen for the hidden feelings of that particular historical period. They tried to convey the social and psychological tensions of their time, the problems of adaptation which a very large number of people were obviously experiencing, and the crisis which seemed to be looming for civilization.

Gustav Mahler is the dominant figure of the contemporary symphonic repertory. He is without doubt the composer who has best communicated the underlying spiritual anguish of European society in the late nineteenth and early twentieth centuries, an anguish that stood in stark contrast with the naïve confidence of the population in sustained material progress and with the official optimism of heads of state, financiers, and entrepreneurs. The problem which obsessed Mahler throughout his life was to reconcile reality as he perceived it within himself, as it were, with the reality which society and the outside world were imposing upon him. He expanded symphonic forms to their limits, not only in duration but also in complexity of detail and transparency of sound.

Another composer of that period, but of an earlier generation, was Johannes Brahms, who felt intimidated by the symphonic structures which to music lovers in the second half of the nineteenth century represented the high point of musical art and of personal expression. It was rather late in his career that he decided to approach that particular form, which gave the new industrial society so much satisfaction and which was in its mind a testimony of its achievements. When Brahms finally overcame his hesitations, his music tended to convey some of the disturbed feelings of the age: disenchantment, resignation, and the yearning for a sense of personal identity.

The symbolic meaning of classical music remains very real in spite of the elitism and the snobbishness which often pervade the concert hall, and no matter whether it is perceived consciously or not. However, English and French in Montreal react to it in very different ways. It is clear that the English community in Montreal identifies much more closely with the economic system than does the French population, which has never really acceded to the top of the largest firms and to the exercise of economic power. Indeed, throughout the modern history of Quebec, the French-speaking elites have often challenged the economic system in order to substitute a new set of values deemed more appropriate to their social and economic circumstances.

Differences in the respective experience and interests of Montreal's two main language groups inevitably affects the manner in which they react to music. Inasmuch as one can generalize about such matters, it would seem that the English-speaking community is more sensitive to the symbolic and mystical aspect of classical music, whereas the French community responds to its aesthetic and cultural aspects.

For these reasons, members of the English-speaking community will involve themselves more readily and will show a greater determination to keep the upper hand in the organization and in the contents of the concerts. Symphonic music represents a sort of psychological extension of its economic and social activities. The French-speaking concert-going public, on the other hand, is more passive in its appreciation of classical music. It considers it to be just an element of general culture without close relationship to the surrounding world, one whose main significance is deeply personal and private. This attitude will incidentally foster class distinctions and elitism.

The barrage of criticism levelled at the management of the Montreal Symphony during the financial crisis of 1973 did not really originate with people who subscribed to concert series. The immediate source was in the realm of politics, particularly among nationalist elements. The ideas behind the criticism were largely inspired by models of popular and democratic control that many nationalists wanted to apply to all aspects of collective life, such as the economy, community services, and so on. Another source was in the demands of Quebec performing artists who were eager to have the orchestra give in to regionalist and nationalist sentiment prevalent at that time, a move which would be to their obvious advantage.

As in numerous other circumstances, the motives which underlie nationalist agitation originate in concerns of an occupational nature which are then projected onto the whole of French society and presented as essential to its survival. The professionals who make up the bulk of the middle class, the intellectuals, and the artists in Quebec have always feared and opposed the establishment of a society open to outside competition and subject to standards of excellence that might threaten the autonomy and the vigour of French cultural life. Quebec would be reduced to the level of a minor North American region with few distinguishing characteristics.

However, there are very definite limits to the capacity of nationalism to influence political developments in French society. Some are set by the very resistance which it arouses among certain elements of the French-speaking population. But the most important limits are internal ones in the sense that they are closely bound to the thought processes of Quebec nationalism itself.

However, a very large number of English-speaking people in Montreal, influenced by profound doubts as to the existence of these limits, experienced panic fear of some destructive and vengeful outburst on the part of those they apparently knew very little about. It is as if they believed that the political tendencies prevailing at the moment, which already seemed so dangerous, would be amplified in a relentless and irreversible process, dragging all of Quebec into excesses that no contrary force could overcome. Of course, the question raised by these fears is that of the psychological equilibrium of the French population.

English-speaking Montreal, at least that part of it which regularly attended symphony concerts, saw a threat to freedom behind the criticisms and the claims addressed to the orchestra during the 1973 crisis. If professional standards governing the hiring of musicians had to be lowered to accommodate more francophones, this would mean the introduction of ideological and even racist considerations in the composition and the operation of the orchestra. Afterwards, there would be nothing to prevent provincial authorities from pushing matters to their bitter end and giving satisfaction to the most militant and extremist demands.

If nationalist considerations were to influence the makeup of the orchestra, it seemed natural that they would also affect its repertory and the commissions awarded to Quebec composers. In such a way, it was feared, musical expression would be subordinated to other considerations having nothing to do with it, putting an end to artistic freedom in music and wherever the interests of society and of nationalism could be served. Political liberties would not survive very long in such a climate of cultural planning and constraint.

This manner of projecting current trends into the future is inspired by some rather terrifying precedents. The English community, which has been feeling attacked and diminished by the social upheaval of the last twenty years or so, cannot always resist the temptation of applying them offensively to the Quebec scene. Nazi Germany once practised this kind of authoritarianism in the name of racial and cultural purity. No moral restraints operated to prevent the crimes of Nazi Germany, which methodically proceeded to do away with the Jewish population. An important percentage of Montreal's English-speaking population happen to be Jews who themselves have survived Nazi extermination camps or have relatives who died there.

In the Soviet Union, it was the establishment of socialism that provided the pretext for authoritarianism in politics and culture. In the 1930s, under Stalin, the official aesthetic doctrine was referred to as "socialist realism." In the realm of music, it consisted in rejecting any composition that did not have the desired popular tone, that is, which showed reprehensible tendencies towards individualism and formalism.

At the present time, Quebec nationalism is clearly identified with social democracy and has very little to do with the authoritarian system which the Nazis built up in Germany and which seems to have been the product of a collective psychosis brought on by the collapse of social values after the First World War and by the devastating inflation which followed. Nor does it have anything to do with an inability to internalize order and discipline for which the Soviet regime is brutally attempting to compensate. Quebec nationalism is of a different nature altogether and pursues objectives which can hardly be equated with those of large European countries.

Thus, insofar as the Montreal orchestra was a political issue, the most extreme proposals simply supported the principle that users should pay, that the government's share of the required funding should henceforth be assumed by concert-goers and by wealthy patrons eager to support this type of cultural endeavour. Yet even this proposal had no audience at all, either in the government or among the public. There could be no question of rejecting symphonic music as somehow foreign to the spirit of French Quebec and of denying its significance for a broadly based culture.

Similarly, there was never any question of transforming symphonic music into a vehicle for national sentiment or for nationalism, as was the case in many European countries during the nineteenth century. This particular role has been taken over by more popular forms of expression. It is assumed mainly by *chansonniers* and by various rock groups, and to a certain extent by film, theatre, and literature. This is to say that nationalism is mostly verbal and that without recognizable emotional equivalents it does not lend itself to nonverbal arts such as classical music, sculpture, and painting. In Quebec, these activities have traditionally been very individualistic and inward-looking, and they have seldom been used for purposes of exhortation. These traits peculiar to Quebec's own sense of culture indicate that nationalism is geared to practical objectives related to protest rather than to ideology, that it seeks to mobilize for down-to-earth objectives rather than to permeate every aspect of collective life.

There is, naturally, an abundant literature described in French as *misérabiliste*, writings which seek political effect by presenting Quebec life as mean and sordid. The best example is Pierre Vallières's *Nègres blancs d'Amérique*, which has been translated into English as *The White Niggers of America*. There is also in politics a pronounced tendency to stress collective wounds such as the Battle of the Plains of Abraham. Nevertheless, in spite of the intensity with which nationalist causes may occasionally be presented, there is no historical trauma susceptible of causing the kind of seizure that occurred in Germany and in Russia.

The idea of subordinating artistic activity to the national interest, a proposition which betrays a taste for authoritarianism, is extremely rare among contemporary Quebec intellectuals and has never been the object of serious political discussion. On the contrary, the prevailing tendency is to insist on the need for preserving creative freedom from outside intervention, particularly that of the state, which most people would like to see as flexible and tolerant as possible in this respect. These, then, are the political and psychological limits of nationalism in Quebec which may be detected through an analysis of the relationship between artists and the surrounding society and the state.

It is always tempting to believe that the creation of a country, the spread of a language, or the exclusive possession of a territory will bring about a solution to the problems of alienation in contemporary society. Many people will speak and act as if the conquest of national identity should coincide with the achievement of personal identity, as if the first automatically gave rise to the second. But this somewhat narrow conception of culture and of its social function is rejected by most Quebec intellectuals. Indeed, to perceive individual development in these terms is a sure way of blocking its progress. Such is the conclusion which Michel Morin and Claude Bertrand reach in *Le territoire imaginaire de la culture*:

> This is why a certain nationalist approach to culture which assigns to this itinerary the reappropriation of national identity can only reproduce the theme of dispossession as the central theme of that culture. This is how one might be led into what we referred to earlier as the aesthetics of powerlessness. But there is no other solution to this state of alienation, which we must not forget is that of the inner life, no other solution than the one which will be discovered, always provisionally, in another world, unreal and interior, the very world of culture which cannot be reduced to a real territory: this is to say that there is no other solution to this state than the one which is ever contingent and which proceeds from the creative effort of the individual.[7]

7. Michel Morin and Claude Bertrand, *Le territoire imaginaire de la culture* (Montréal: Hurtubise HMH, 1979), p. 116.

The Nation-State
and Independence

The achievement of the nation-state is the ultimate objective with which the Parti Québécois has been identified since its foundation in 1968 and which it has inherited from its predecessor, the Ralliement pour l'indépendance nationale. This concept, which can be translated into different forms of political sovereignty, has fostered the revival and the modernization of nationalist thinking in Quebec. It was by rallying behind the idea of the nation-state that nationalists were able at last to accept the urban and industrial society which for such a long time had appeared to them as a threat to French cultural survival.

Until the time of the Quiet Revolution, nationalist elites exhibited contradictory attitudes towards North American capitalism. On the one hand, they had to recognize its beneficial effects on their standard of living. But on the other, they felt the need to react strongly to some of its harmful consequences, against which there was really no satisfactory defence. The organization of industrial production introduced to everyday life new centres of interest which came in conflict with the group solidarity characteristic of French society. The loyalty which large corporations required from their employees, plus the possibilities of upward mobility which they seemed to offer, helped undermine the traditional values to which the rural and agricultural mentalities were still attached and which they fought desperately to preserve.

The compromise which survived for more than a century rested on the social and political isolation of rural society. This voluntary isolation helped minimize the corrosive effects of capitalism and reduce to the bare minimum participation in the rival industrial society that was taking shape in urban centres; but at the same time it did not totally cut French society off from the advantages which industrial work brought to the people and to the economy.

The psychological cost associated with this ambivalent attitude was extremely heavy. In order to justify a willingly accepted economic dependence on English capitalists, it was necessary to perpetuate the old notion of ethnic callings according to which one group was believed gifted for business and the other for cultural endeavours. However, this ethnic division of labour, so to speak, could hardly survive without the French internalizing unfavourable English prejudices about themselves, that is, without their accepting the idea of their incompetence in certain fields, particularly business.

This negative self-image surfaces in the works of numerous writers at different periods of Quebec history. It also lurks in the background of most political discussions and is conveyed most clearly whenever national independence is being discussed. Even nationalists, and perhaps they most of all, gave expression to this view. Edmond de Nevers, considered one of the precursors of the nationalist movement which appeared after the First World War and which was led by Lionel Groulx, indulged in this national self-criticism in *L'avenir du peuple canadien-français*, published in Paris in 1896:

> As for the independence of Quebec, it would be ridiculous even to think about it. It would mean the establishment of a republic on the South American model; it would open the gates to every appetite, every ambition, and every vanity, and establish in a permanent way the reign of corruption, of mediocrity, and of intolerance.[1]

The humiliating self-image which French society sometimes projects is also expressed in modern terms by mem-

1. Quoted by Claude Galarneau in *Edmond de Nevers, essayiste* (Québec: Les Presses de l'Université Laval, 1969), p. 62 (author's translation).

bers of the moderate left to which the nationalist movement belongs. Taking their rhetoric from Third World political writers, they deplore the powerlessness of colonized people— that is, themselves—to achieve liberation from the foreign rulers who determine the main orientations of their collective life. The whole period extending from the onset of the Quiet Revolution to the referendum on sovereignty-association in May 1980 is presented as a long attempt to formulate a national purpose and identity.

The concrete form which this quest must eventually assume is that of the nation-state. Quebec's relations with Canada, the United States, France, and other countries of the world could conceivably be conducted in a situation of complete independence or of sovereignty-association, or even within the framework of some voluntary participation in a renewed federal system. But for the last twenty years, as a result of some curious political illusion, attention has focused almost exclusively on the state, its role, and its powers, while the existence of the nation was taken for granted by everybody.

Yet during the Quiet Revolution in the 1960s, the government of Quebec had assumed many of if not most of the powers associated with an independent state, this within the constitutional limits imposed by the British North America Act. While it lacked actual independence, it had the capacity for it. The Deposit and Investment Fund, which manages contributions to the Quebec Pension Plan, assumed a role analogous in many respects to that of a central bank. The department of intergovernmental affairs began to resemble a ministry of foreign affairs as it established various contacts with foreign governments under the suspicious eyes of federal authorities. For quite some time, and unlike most Canadian provinces, Quebec had had its own provincial police force. Finally, with its able and numerous public service, the government of Quebec was ready to assume any constitutional role that voters might choose for it; all that was needed was to turn the key.

In the fusion of two distinct concepts into that of the nation-state, it was actually the nation that failed. Although the people of Quebec are consistently described as constituting a true nation, there was obvious dissatisfaction and disappointment with it. The most passionate supporters of independence, along with those that the Parti Québécois had brought together in the name of social democracy, worked hard to elevate the nation to the level of the state they had in mind and which was precisely the one which had been built during the Quiet Revolution. By the intensity of their political involvement, they sought to make up for the lack of cohesion which the people of Quebec seemed to exhibit. All the agitation and the tensions which plagued the successive governments of Daniel Johnson, Jean-Jacques Bertrand, and Robert Bourassa resulted from the search for an illusory unanimity.

Throughout the whole period between the 1966 and the Parti Québécois' accession to power in 1976, there was a high degree of collective anxiety originating in the deep and rapid transformations which had shaken Quebec in the preceding decades: the unexpected drop in the birth rate, the collapse of the social and even spiritual influence of the Catholic Church, the appearance of the welfare state and of its intrusive bureaucracy, and, especially, the acceptance of the social values related to urbanization and to advanced industrialization. In spite of the visible progress achieved during this period, there were widespread feelings of impending crisis. The collective future seemed unsure and not very promising. People were expecting the worst.

At the very moment when French Quebec was acceding to industrial capitalism through the financial and technical means put together by the provincial government, and just when the intellectual elite was assuming the leadership of a movement for national liberation, there appeared a very serious obstacle to the circulation of ideas and to the realization of political unanimity among the population. That obstacle was the degraded state of vernacular language.

Up until the middle of the nineteenth century, there were few differences in the language spoken by the well-to-do and educated classes and the bulk of the population. All evidence points to similarity of accent, syntax, and even vocabulary.

The language spoken by different classes belonged to the same psychological universe. No social barriers based on language intervened in the meeting of minds at times of political crisis such as the Rebellion of 1837 or the Act of Union of 1840; everything occurred spontaneously.

But industrialization, brought on by English-speaking managers with monopoly access to capital and technology, introduced an element of division that could not be suppressed. Lacking a French vocabulary with which to describe the new industrial activities, the new type of organization, and the new economic realities, popular language was overtaken by words and expressions drawn directly from English. Apprenticeship into the industrial society of the nineteenth century caused the syntax of the spoken language to be modelled closely on that of English. Ultimately, educated and working classes came to speak in ways that differed considerably and were closely attuned to the occupational and economic situation of each.

Class distinctions resulting from differences in language were added to those fostered by the negative attitude of educated people towards business activities and to the social control which firms sought to maintain over the activities of their own employees and the working class as a whole. In this situation, after 1860, the Church and the clergy emerged as the leading agents of national unity among the French in Quebec. It was they who helped preserve the fundamental unity and understanding among the classes.

In the aftermath of the Quiet Revolution, while the influence of the Church was on the wane and nationalist sentiment became more prominent, there were fears that class distinctions would compromise the solidarity and the cohesion necessary for the achievement of the nation-state and of national independence. Réal Caouette and the Créditiste movement had already demonstrated the existence of very deep political divisions. The fear was that they would inevitably grow into social and cultural ones, and eventually prove to be insurmountable.

Nationalists felt instinctively that the situation was moving in a direction that might prove threatening for the historical egalitarianism and for the democratic sentiments which gave French Quebec its originality and its unique character. Some vague and ill-defined apprehension was felt about the ultimate fate of Quebec's collective identity, whose roots plunged some three hundred years into the past. Specifically, the danger was that widening class divisions would threaten the political unanimity which had allowed the French to maintain their common front against the wealthier and more powerful English, and to ensure their survival in the most unfavourable circumstances and without any economic power whatsoever. Political life in Quebec, in the later 1960s and early 1970s, became morose as it had never been before.

There were continual attempts to restore the basic unity of French society and to repel English cultural penetration. Most of them were inspired by the traditional response that consisted in encouraging the isolation of the French population from the rest of the English-speaking continent. At the end of the eighteenth century and at the beginning of the nineteenth, the seigneurial regime offered an effective defence because of its system of land tenure inspired from feudalism and unsuited to capitalist accumulation. Later, during the second half of the nineteenth century, isolation was the product of clerical authoritarianism and ultramontane Catholicism. In one case as in the other, an educated elite was seeking to consolidate its preeminent status and its hold over the population by making itself the eager promoter of that society's originality and of everything that could set it off from all others.

It is in this context that *joual* enjoyed a curious career. The word refers to a type of spoken French which spread with industrialization and which is heavily indebted to elementary English technical terms. *Joual* became a political issue in 1959 at the end of the Duplessis regime. It acquired high visibility when André Laurendeau, editor of *Le Devoir*, put forward the argument that national revival after years of relative stagnation would have to rest on a steady improvement of spoken and written French. A year later, Jean-Paul Desbiens published *Les insolences du frère Untel* which described *joual* as a degenerate form of thought which served only to perpetuate collective powerlessness. This dialect of the industrial age was believed to be a prelude to anglicization since it could only flourish because of a general loss of motivation towards a purer and more literate form of French. At the time, everyone agreed with this diagnosis.

But a few years later, certain Quebec writers began to make use of *joual* in plays and novels. Prominent among them were Gérald Godin and Michel Tremblay. They had various reasons for doing this, the main one being a preoccupation with realism. However, it did not take long for the use of *joual* to become a political gesture. In this case, the basic idea was to remain in close communion and to display one's solidarity with the people. Some, like Henri Bélanger, even wanted to make *joual* into a language of communication and culture proper to Quebec. Left-wing nationalists saw the use of correct and literary French as a symptom of bourgeois aspirations.

The nature of *joual* underwent a radical transformation after it was appropriated by nationalist elements. It had originally been a sort of industrial patois or dialect spoken in working-class districts by those who had been uprooted from their former rural occupations and who were least educated, poorest, and most demoralized. However, starting in the late 1960s, it was eagerly cultivated by a whole generation of politicized students. They used it aggressively as the symbol of a classless society, which was the new object taken by the traditional and historical yearning for an egalitarian society.

Some left-wing politicians and trade unionists, such as Michel Chartrand, identified spontaneously with *joual* and made persistent and opportunistic use of it. The intention was obviously to bridge the widening gap between educated people and the working class. It was hoped that ideological and social control would be made easier by speaking a type of language whose popular roots would be perceived as a sign of sincerity and authenticity.

But the psychological advantages of *joual* faded abruptly after the Parti Québécois' accession to power in 1976. The first action of the new government was the adoption of Bill 101, which made French the only official language of Quebec. The law was accompanied by a statement of broad cultural goals, one of which happened to be the improvement of the spoken and written language in the province. At that point *joual* ceased being an instrument of social and political struggle. It reverted to what it had long represented: a minor but embarrassing manifestation of Quebec regionalism.

The desire to recover the ancient pre-industrial egalitarianism expressed itself through the growing use of Marxist dialectics in the trade union movement and in the universities. The concepts of class struggle, economic exploitation, and social revolution came to occupy a central place in the strategy of collective bargaining as well as in political discourses. For a large number of intellectuals, Marxist theory provided a new way of presenting nationalist claims and of preserving the historical relationship between the educated elites and the bulk of the population.

What sets the labour movement in Quebec apart from other unions in North America is the fact that its leaders rarely emerge from the ranks but are for the most part university graduates and intellectuals eager to participate in movements for social reform. This is particularly true of the home-grown Confederation of National Trade Unions, which until 1960 used to grant official status within its ranks to Catholic chaplains. It is therefore remarkable how, after turning its back on Catholicism in favour of socialism, the CNTU has hardly needed to modify the relations it has always had with working-class people in general.

Today, as in former times, union leaders act as if being part of the working class is a sort of prison from which there is no escape. People in Montreal used to say of one of the city's working-class neighbourhoods, "If you are born in Saint-Henri, you die in Saint-Henri." This was a way of pointing to the rigidity of class barriers, which in Quebec rest mostly on educational disparities. The conception of unionism practised by the CNTU, formerly known as the Canadian and Catholic Confederation of Labour, or "Catholic syndicates," was one of missionary work concerned with justice instead of religion. As is the case with the socialist viewpoint of today, there was no attempt to sway people from their awareness of class, to promote upward mobility, or to upset traditional social stratification. On the contrary, unionism then and now perpetuated a kind of social fatalism which served only to reinforce the system.

As the Confederation of National Trade Unions gradually became more militant in its outlook, a new political objective appeared: the establishment of socialism to provide the working class with a determining influence on the organization of economic activity. In this context, the labour movement believes itself to be the true guardian of the faith, the only one authorized to look after the social and economic education of its members. Out of jealousy and exclusiveness, it eagerly seeks to promote feelings of class and to put a damper on the kind of individualism that could undermine the efficiency of the movement. The CNTU professes to be at war with what it calls *le syndicalisme d'affaires*, business-oriented unionism, which it associates with the rival Quebec Federation of Labour, a loosely structured organization including provincial sections of Canadian and international unions. These unions generally support the present economic system, they do not offer any coherent ideology leading to political action, and they are content with demands relating almost exclusively to wages and general working conditions.

The CNTU's European approach stands out against North American attitudes and against those of a large proportion of people in Quebec. Most workers do not feel any loyalty to occupations whose contents are constantly being modified by technology and inflation. They do not feel bound by their status and their working-class ties. The prospects of upward social mobility for oneself and one's family, even if they are not as rosy as is generally thought, are part of North American reality. Unionism then becomes a question of self-interest rather than of ideology. Working-class solidarity helps sustain the advancement of individuals rather than the power of a particular class. This is to say that workers' solidarity and class sentiment, both of which happen to be very strong in Quebec, are not linked with political goals as far as the majority are concerned.

The groups who responded most readily to attempts at social and ideological control were those for whom union action had already proved to be the most economically and professionally beneficial: public-service employees, particularly in education and health care. Many categories of non-management employees have acquired, through collective bargaining with public authorities, the recognition of a sort of monopoly in the application of knowledge to certain tasks and occupations, rights similar in spirit to those conferred in a more formal way by the Bar Association or the College of Physicians. It is among these groups newly integrated into a social and professional hierarchy that one finds the most ardent nationalists and those who are most inclined to defend Quebec's traditional social structures.

Of all the attempts made to bring Quebec outside the mainstream of North America the most spectacular was that of the Front de Libération du Québec. During the 1960s, the FLQ concentrated on bombings, holdups, and thefts of arms, with few victims and little property damage. While public opinion was vocal in its condemnation of violence, it nevertheless rejoiced in the political effects it seemed to have on the use of the French language in business and industry and on the sharing of power between Quebec and Ottawa. However, tension suddenly rose in October 1970 with the kidnapping of the British commercial attaché in Montreal, James R. Cross; and it reached an almost intolerable level with the kidnapping and the murder of Pierre Laporte, labour minister in the government of Robert Bourassa.

The death of Pierre Laporte had a profound and unpredictable effect on political trends in Quebec and it contributed to a further widening of the gulf between the intellectuals and the bulk of the population. Many intellectuals exhibited a certain tolerance and indulgence towards revolutionary violence, to which they compared the violence of the capitalist system. According to the inclinations displayed by various groups, the death of a man was seen as an unfortunate accident, a peripheral incident in the struggle against foreign domination, or an exemplary fate for all those participating in one way or another in national repression. The idea of armed struggle, even if it was not explicitly endorsed, acquired a romantic aura which, many thought, could help mobilize the hearts and minds of the people.

Among the general population, however, the death of Pierre Laporte had an entirely different impact. It meant, in the very tense climate of that period, that violence was taking a new and different course by choosing a victim who happened to be a French Canadian. This sudden turn was antagonistic to the historical cohesion and the national solidarity which had enabled French culture, ever since the Battle of the Plains of Abraham, to survive the assimilating pressures of English. It was as if the intellectual elite had severed its ties with the people. The latter's immediate reaction was to rally round Prime Minister Pierre Trudeau who, in spite of the excessive character of the War Measures Act, became the protector of the fundamental unity of French society as well as a rampart against the destructive excesses of left-wing nationalists.

The unhealthy climate associated with the events of October 1970 persisted until 1976 when the Parti Québécois came to power. There was at that moment a general sigh of relief, as if a long-standing political crisis had just been resolved. The feelings of optimism and confidence which surfaced at that moment were shared even by those who had just been thrown out of office and who were somewhat disturbed by the various projects of the new government concerning independence, language, and culture.

The very first law proposed by Premier René Lévesque's new government, on the status of the French language, was designed to affirm its nationalist ideology and to define the cultural characteristics of the Quebec nation. The achievement of a national state, which required nothing more than popular sanction by a referendum, was postponed. It seemed as if the whole question of cultural identity should be given priority over the creation of new political structures, that the resolution of cultural problems was to be the prelude for the resolution of the political ones.

The Parti Québécois, highly alert to the linguistic tensions which had been poisoning political life, thus went into action immediately with a law on language. French Canada's obvious desire to participate as an equal partner in the management of the country's economic life, and to acquire access to the main centres of decision, was the ultimate stage of a profound cultural revolution which had been foreshadowed twenty years earlier by the sharp and unexpected decline in the birth rate. The tardy acceptance of economic realities worked in such a way as to reduce the social and cultural differences between French and English. A point was reached where language was almost the only important factor of differentiation between the two groups. It was therefore on the very issue of language that public opinion in Quebec displayed the greatest degree of agitation in the decade preceding the Parti Québécois' rise to power.

The most controversial aspects of the new legislation concerned education, where access to English schools was denied to any child whose parents had not received an English education in Quebec. This restriction, putting an end to the freedom of choice which had traditionally been the rule, was inspired by feelings of anxiety in the face of the steady decline in the birth rate and the massive integration of immigrants into Montreal's English community. Public opinion insisted on countermeasures to check the proportional decline of French-speaking people in Canada and of their representation in federal institutions. Public authorities came under relentless pressure to forestall the possibility that Montreal, the heart of the provincial economy, might one day cease to be a French city.

The law's provisions on education helped divert towards the French community countless members of Montreal's ethnic groups who until then had sought economic success and social advancement by learning to speak English and integrating into the English community. But justification for that aspect of the law rested to a large extent on a somewhat improper use of demographic data and on ignorance of the inner workings of large Canadian corporations. The authors of the law seemed to believe that the preponderance of English in trade and industry rested mainly on the number of people who happened to have English as their language. A reading of demographic projections led them to believe that one day soon the French character and traditions of Montreal would be completely submerged by English influence.

But these fears are somewhat exaggerated if one considers that the very favourable situation of English in Quebec is due just as much to the Anglo-Protestant monopoly of the leading posts in large Canadian corporations as to the number of English-speaking people who actually live in Montreal. There was a time when executives and managers were recruited locally. Since the Second World War, however, this has become insufficient, and Montreal-based firms must tap the human resources of the whole country. This new situation is partly explained by economic growth and bureaucratic expansion. But one must also take into account the fact that the Anglo-Protestant minority, which occupies the top of the social pyramid, has systematically excluded other ethnic groups from the management of large Canadian corporations and of the national economy. This minority, instead of accepting within its ranks members of other groups such as Jews or Italians, has insisted on preserving its exclusivity. Because Anglo-Protestant recruiting and promotion has now become difficult, the trend in Montreal has been towards the gradual francization of company operations starting from the bottom and moving towards the top. Independently of the corporate migration towards Toronto and points west, economic power is being abandoned to the French majority who will eventually impose their own language on business in the province.

The francization of business is, incidentally, another objective of the Parti Québécois' language legislation. However, even this is perceived as a cultural rather than an economic conquest in the sense that its basic purpose is to broaden and diversify the scope of French activities. The impact of francization on the economy and on the internal organization of business firms attracts very little interest. Attention tends to focus on the satisfaction of traditional nationalist demands such as the expansion of personal horizons and the end of a form of discrimination which prevented French-speaking people from acceding to the decision-making centres of the economy.

Naturally enough, those who were adversely affected by the law tried to draw attention to the ill effects that francization of corporate management might have on the provincial economy. Public opinion was generally unmoved by the self-serving arguments of the English community, but it proved impossible to ignore the hostile reactions which the law produced outside Quebec. French public opinion, however, being poorly informed on economic matters, concerned itself solely with the political aspects of the issue: it rejoiced in the aggressive pursuit of French interests but was somewhat dismayed by the political caution that had become necessary. This helps to explain the equivocal and ambiguous attitudes revealed in subsequent public opinion polls whereby respondents expressed satisfaction with government policy while stating their intentions of voting for the Liberal opposition.

Yet the Parti Québécois government was rather moderate and prudent as regards business. Its nationalism was purely cultural and did not seek to alter existing economic structures or the legal system which governed them. The party's version of independence, while moving forward on the francization of business activity in Quebec, was meant to preserve the integrity of Canada's economic territory with the concept of sovereignty-association.

The introduction of the so-called Charter of the French Language in the National Assembly was accompanied by a broad policy statement in which the government explained why it was pushed into action. After describing the critical situation of French in Canada and in Quebec, the document stated some broad explanatory principles. The first was: "In Quebec, the French language is not only a means of expression, it is a way of life." Such a statement was meant to stress the changes that had taken place in official thinking on questions of language. Ten years earlier, Premier Daniel Johnson had merely raised the possibility of regulating language use in some way, as had already been done for "other means of communication." But for the Parti Québécois, regulation was to be part of a process of cultural maturation.

> The idea is to protect and foster in its fullness an original culture: a mode of being, thinking, writing, coming together, establishing relations between groups and individuals, and even conducting business. This requirement, with its countless implications, goes beyond the technical process of translation: it cannot possibly be met simply because someone has condescended to prepare a French terminology for realities which remain fundamentally foreign or hostile. It is not a linguistic problem that the daily use of such words as "hot-dog" or "banana-split" will pose: it is a problem of culture. If the point of it all were merely to demand that a foreign way of life be servilely rendered into French words, who could possibly be interested in it, or opposed?[2]

The question which this statement raises, but which it does not really answer, is how one should define a culture that is proper to French Quebec. What precisely are the characteristics of this mode of being and of thinking that must absolutely be protected against foreign influence, in this case that of English-speaking North America? To what extent do the values associated with it constitute an inalienable fund that no outside influence should be allowed to alter? These are questions that have received different answers at various moments in history. There was a time when royal authority, first French and then British, constituted an integral element of national

2. *La politique québécoise de la langue française* (Québec: Gouvernement du Québec, Editeur officiel, 1977), pp. 21–22 (author's translation).

life. Later, the population came to identify its culture with a system of land tenure inspired from feudalism and with a legal system derived from the common law of Paris, in order to resist the encroachments of English capitalism.

Starting from the second half of the nineteenth century, the Catholic faith was the foundation of national consciousness. One of its ideological extensions was the idea of a rural and agricultural society placed under the benevolent authority of religious, professional, and political elites. These elites openly practised a moral and cultural protectionism of which Abbé Lionel Groulx, a leading exponent of traditional nationalist thinking, was the most ardent defender. Constantly invoking an image of masters who must protect the moral health of their students, Groulx provided the basic outline of a cultural policy. His views exerted considerable influence on the nationalist thought that emerged from the Quiet Revolution, but they happened to be a source of great confusion because of their incompatibility with the goals of a society that also wanted to be industrial, democratic, and pluralistic:

It is in the name of the original culture, in order to safeguard it, that they [the teachers] claim for themselves the right to impose certain prohibitions. It is the same for a nation as for any living organism: inoculation of an element that cannot be assimilated introduces the principle of death into its life. Therefore, should one hold it against our teachers if they have refused to allow certain foreigners, certain aliens—no matter how illustrious—to become the gods of our nation's youth because they wanted to prevent Germanic or Slavic fogs from snuffing out the clarity of our Latin minds? To state matters directly, we have no use for any work and any aesthetic principle which do not serve French culture and which therefore cannot be considered to be art and cannot create any.[3]

3. Lionel Groulx, "Une action intellectuelle," L'Action française 1, no. 2 (February 1917): 39 (author's translation).

One must note that Groulx attributes to the word culture a more restricted meaning than is generally given today. For him, culture represents only intellectual activities and interests, faith and customs being set in separate compartments. Nowadays, under the influence of secularization and of sociological thinking, culture comprises all intellectual activities and behaviour in a given society. For Groulx, cultural life must be subject to religious models:

> The time is no more when literature could be considered an inoffensive diversion. Our whole literary tradition cries out against this kind of dilettantism. With us, to write is to live, to defend one's self, and to endure. As the incarnation of a thought and of a life, the work of art encloses the soul of a race within an immortal form, thereby becoming a virtual principle of duration. And this, it seems to us, shows our intellectual workers the urgency of their duty. Let them consider that all determination takes its source in an intellectual impulse; that any liberating movement proceeds from the intellectuals to the crowd.[4]

Many things have changed since this was written more than sixty years ago. But contemporary nationalists, gathered in the Parti Québécois, are still having considerable difficulty in extricating themselves from the influence of Abbé Groulx, particularly as regards those concepts inspired by the conditions and attitudes of his age. For Groulx, authoritarianism, elitism, the adoption of a monolithic ideology, cultural exclusivity, all were natural ways of being and of thinking, accepted without question. But matters are very different today. This is quite apparent within the Parti Québecois, where attempts have been made through the concept of sovereignty-association to adapt to the liberal society and the economic organization of North America.

As a result of the modernization pursued in Quebec for almost a generation, mentalities have been transformed and have adapted themselves to new situations. Authoritarianism

4. Ibid., pp. 34–35.

and paternalism have practically disappeared and given way to manipulation. Elitism is no longer acceptable and what remains of it has gone underground, so to speak, and operates in more informal guises. But the acceptance of the type of pluralism basic to liberal society is sometimes rather painful. Thus the government as well as the population give the impression of being torn between two irreconcilable worlds. Like all other communities, Quebec exhibits attitudes and behaviours clinging to the past while straining towards the future.

The distrust of pluralism, which is almost a conditioned reflex, is deeply rooted and persists in spite of the trend towards more open attitudes. Historically, the Catholic Church has always encouraged a form of religious segregation. It continues to do so even though serious problems have cropped up in some French-language schools in Montreal. As a result of the government's language legislation they are the only schools available to immigrant children of diverse religious backgrounds. But in a pastoral letter dealing with this issue, Archbishop Paul Grégoire of Montreal wrote that he would prefer the establishment of a distinct nondenominational system for non-Catholics to the prospect of what he called "debilitating relativism" in the educational system.

The fear of debilitating relativism has also gripped a large number of educators and parents who are energetically opposed to the early teaching of English as a second language. The reason advanced is that this may affect a child's ability to handle the syntax and the vocabulary of his mother tongue. There is also strong opposition, for fear of adverse effects on the quality of the spoken language, to the idea that French- and English-speaking students should, in some areas and for economy's sake, share the same facilities and premises. There are countless comparable situations where this kind of defence mechanism springs into action and enforces a policy of isolation. The Parti Québécois' language legislation, Bill 101, simply suppresses one of the threatening elements by placing an interdict on English-language signs.

That legislation, which seems to have received the support of most French-speaking people, was the high-water mark of nationalist pressure, which had been increasingly strong since the early 1960s. By imposing French as the language of every field, including business, the government caused the disappearance of the old constricting frontiers within which French culture had long survived. So vivid was the feeling of relief after the sudden expansion of the psychological territory occupied by French culture that serious questions are raised about the real intent of nationalist agitation which had been dominant right up to that moment.

Was the ultimate purpose really to prevent the French population from becoming a minority within Quebec as suggested by many demographic projections, supported by countless political speeches? Or was the prevailing feeling of suffocation due not so much to pressures from the outside but from the threat of internal collapse? Had Quebec arrived at a critical situation whereby French society could no longer survive without a greater diversity than that allowed by its old social and economic boundaries? This might explain some of the aggressive and vengeful aspects of the language legislation which go against the generally tolerant and conciliatory attitudes of the French-speaking population.

Whatever the case may be, the application of Bill 101 brought about a perceptible change in voter expectations of the Parti Québécois. It was as if there had been an unconscious decision that the language legislation had first to be digested before the launching of some new enterprise likely to result in fundamental transformations. It was as if the majority had turned its back on those aspects of nationalism which aim at collective isolation from English-speaking North America, and as if a genuine desire for closer contacts with English-speaking North America had come to the fore as a result of the greater security afforded by the language legislation. Its adoption in 1977 soon gave rise to the first attempt at ideological and cultural reconciliation with English Canada and with the United States.

In the policy statement that accompanied the presentation of Bill 101 in the National Assembly, the government indicated that its goal was a purer culture that would exclude undesirable English influences and reflect a French historical past. One might have expected the government to act on its own intentions and bring together the financial and legal means for putting its long-term objectives into effect. However, it became apparent in 1978, with the publication of *La politique québécoise du développement culturel*, that the government had retreated from this position, thereby disappointing all those who had expected an energetic continuation of the language policy. While giving plenty of satisfaction to bureaucratic appetites for meddling in every field of human endeavour, the document nevertheless held to a strictly liberal view of society. "The state, as may easily be verified, has no intention of substituting itself either for citizens freely building their culture or for 'quality of life' proponents. The state merely wants to show its solidarity and measure its own responsibilities in this concrete and extensive field of culture."[5]

In other words, the government was to assume only a supportive role. There was no question at all of planning and direct intervention. The document's conclusions make this clear:

We have repeatedly said so: in devising a cultural policy, the state wants first of all to restore the power of citizens to shape their own culture. By making assistance available and by creating various public bodies responsible for its distribution, the state wants to encourage creative freedom, whatever form it might take. Thus we have dealt at length with the collective conditions necessary for cultural development. The state has little to say about the nature of the novel or of film in Quebec; but it can see to it that novels find their place in bookstores and that the films are shown in movie theatres. On a broader scale, in such areas as leisure, work, communications, and education, and in others as well, the state can ensure that proper conditions will

5. *La politique québécoise du développement culturel* (Québec: Gouvernement du Québec, Editeur officiel, 1978), 2: 152 (author's translation).

exist to allow everyone to accede to a creative culture of which the works of artists are the most obvious symbols.[6]

La politique québécoise du développement culturel represents a viewpoint diametrically opposed to that formulated much earlier by Lionel Groulx. The definition given to culture is far more democratic and individualistic, less authoritarian and elitist. It is fairly close to the attitudes of English-speaking people in North America. It seems to be inspired from that philosophical liberalism which nationalism in Quebec had consistently opposed as being inimical to the preservation of French-Canadian values.

This ideological realignment also includes acceptance of economic liberalism, which North American society supports without necessarily putting into effect. There too, the reconciliation is contrary to the historical instincts of Quebec nationalism, which has always feared that economic individualism would eventually undermine the solidarity and the egalitarianism on which the survival of the group was thought to depend. The Parti Québécois has tried not to move too far away from American society and has even been eager to remain as close to it as possible in every possible way save that of language.

Ever since its foundation, the Parti Québécois has tried to minimize the break which independence would inevitably cause with the rest of Canada and the United States. The concept of sovereignty-association, put forward by René Lévesque as early as 1967, was designed to make practical and relevant the old utopian dream of independence. The pains the party took to be as reassuring as possible were therefore very helpful in taking power in November 1976.

In spite of the considerable animosity which the government's language legislation triggered among English-speaking people across the country, the Parti Québécois continued in its desire to be reassuring to all. In this respect, the policy referred to as *l'étapisme* — independence by easy stages — had some rather curious political effects.

6. Ibid., p. 463.

Feeling that time was on his side, Premier René Lévesque sought to dissociate the controversial project of sovereignty from the day-to-day business of government. His reasoning was that voters satisfied with the handling of public affairs would eventually rally to his views on sovereignty-association. To strengthen this probability and to demonstrate that nobody would be taken by surprise, the government thought of first seeking a mandate to negotiate that option with the rest of Canada and then to seek another mandate to implement the agreement that would supposedly be arrived at. But these calculations did not yield the anticipated results.

This manner of getting around the apprehensions of the voters on a political adventure whose outcome they could not foresee had two main consequences. The first was to dissociate the idea of independence from people's everyday experience and interests. The second was to push it back into the ideal realm where it had been nurtured for the greater part of Quebec's political history. Consequently, it became increasingly difficult to sustain the enthusiasm of party organizers and workers. The quality of their commitment to the cause dissipated rather quickly, as did their numbers. Subsequently, in a series of byelections, the government found it impossible to hold its own against a revitalized Liberal party. The majority of voters seemed to be turning their backs on the political project that had been in preparation for a decade.

The results of the referendum held on 20 May 1980 confirmed, as they were expected to, that public opinion had failed to rally behind the government's constitutional plans. The Parti Québécois, however, was not disposed to look objectively at the causes of its defeat. It attributed enormous importance to the way in which federalist supporters had allegedly intimidated the voters with economic arguments against the viability of an independent Quebec. Some also blamed the outcome of the referendum on supporters of gradualism who, out of a desire to be reassuring, had watered down the party program to a point where it failed to inspire confidence and enthusiasm.

The proclamation of independence, even accompanied by an economic union with the rest of Canada, would constitute for most people an extremely serious decision and would represent a wrenching break with the past. Such a step would be justified not by a desire to resolve the countless grievances accumulated against the English-speaking majority in Canada but rather by the firm intention of transforming the existing social and economic order in the province. But, as the Parti Québécois itself recognized in its cultural policies and in the softening of its sovereignty-association project, nothing of the kind could be detected among the vast majority of voters. Indeed, there was an obvious desire to participate even more fully in the spirit and the material benefits of North American civilization.

It was possibly the government's language legislation which, by suddenly enhancing the economic value of French, did the most to restore among the voters more positive feelings towards Canada. Through some strange political process, the law contributed in easing the collective drive towards isolation which generally appears in times of crisis, and it encouraged more intense participation in North American life. This was an effect of the law that no one could have foreseen.

Consequently, the nation did not come together with the state into the new political entity that the Parti Québécois had planned. It continued to perceive its existence as located outside government structures, and as surviving independently of the legal system governing it. The advent of the nation-state, therefore, never took place.

Emergence of the Antinationalists

For fifteen years and more, Pierre Trudeau has been the embodiment of antinationalist sentiment in Quebec. Determined opposition to the autonomist course pursued by the provincial government of Jean Lesage in the spirit of the Quiet Revolution was one of the principal factors which led him to federal politics in 1965. He hoped to become an effective counterforce against the growing nationalism of the middle class and to stop the separatist movement, which was increasingly vocal and aggressive. The weakness of the federal government led by Lester Pearson, which had only minority support in the House of Commons, represented a dangerous situation for both Quebec and Canada.

His thinking, which is highly polemical and geared to political confrontation, is largely inspired by the great nineteenth-century liberal thinkers such as Lord Acton in England and Alexis de Tocqueville in France. His antinationalism is in reality a profound distrust of state authority, which is constantly seeking to appropriate for its own purposes the broad ideological movements expressed by the general population in various societies. These are sentiments which constantly recur in his writings and which provide the foundation for his political statements, even the most extreme and outrageous:

> I know very well that the idea of the nation-state is not solely responsible for the evils of war; modern technology certainly has a great deal to do with it! But the important point is that this idea is responsible for the fact that wars have become more and more *total* in the last two centuries; it is therefore this idea that I am fighting here. Moreover,

every time the state has been founded on some exclusive
and intolerant idea (religion, nation, ideology), this idea has
been the cause of war. Historically, religion has had to
cease being the foundation of the state before the ugly wars
of religion could come to an end. International wars will
end only when the nation ceases to be the foundation of the
state.[1]

According to the prime minister, there is a persistent contradiction between democracy and nationalism, one being the
negation of the other. In accordance with this view, he has
sought to mobilize public opinion against the idea of nationalism:

A democratic government cannot be "nationalistic" because
it must promote the welfare of all citizens without refer-
ence to their ethnic origins. The virtue which a democratic
government will encourage and raise to the level of a principle is that of civic-mindedness and never nationalism;
there will undoubtedly be occasions when a government
will make laws that will benefit various ethnic groups and
will benefit the majority group proportionately to its numbers; but this will happen as a consequence of the equality
of all and not as the right of the strongest.[2]

Making use of his powers and influence as prime minister
and party leader, Pierre Trudeau has worked to counteract
nationalist tendencies towards economic and social isolationism. By promoting a more prominent French presence in federal institutions, he tried to offer national sentiment a creative
outlet which would prevent its politicization and its exclusive
identification with provincial institutions. His political activities seemed founded on the conviction that French Quebec
did not have the population or the intellectual and material

1. Pierre Elliott Trudeau, Le fédéralisme et la société canadienne-française
    (Montréal: Editions Hurtubise HMH, 1967), p. 167 (author's trans-
    lation).
2. Ibid., p. 178.

resources to do without the contribution of the rest of the country and to survive outside the federal system.

The prime minister's behaviour in politics seems based on the belief that ideas have an existence of their own. Some of them, particularly the ones he is fiercely opposed to, apparently possess a corrupting influence which could conceivably infect all of society. They must be fought energetically, though not necessarily with recourse to censorship or repression. And so he has done. The desired outcome of the struggle is to crush any antagonistic attitude with dialectical arguments, as if it were a manifestation of heresy. Pierre Trudeau's thought thereby acquires an adversarial and conflictive character which explains the very unusual nature of his venture into politics.

Although founded on the classical liberalism of the nineteenth century, the prime minister's thinking is lacking one of its key elements. As an ideology and a political system, liberalism requires almost absolute confidence in the mental health and equilibrium of society. Should doubts arise concerning the self-regulating capacity of society, it can be paralysed or rendered completely unstable. In other words, liberalism cannot accept a Manichean view of the world according to which all good resides on one side and evil on the other, contending with each other until one eventually triumphs.

The federal government and the Liberal Party of Canada are involved in a political and ideological crusade against Quebec nationalism as if the latter, were it left unchecked, would necessarily lead to disaster. Nationalism is being fought with a moralizing stance very reminiscent of that formerly used to fight alcoholism or communism. The struggle is being waged with such intensity that after a decade it has produced an obsessive preoccupation with federalism and independence. As very often happens in this type of confrontation, each side becomes very much like the other and political doctrines tend to lose whatever intellectual content they may have had before.

Initially, the conflict was over the integrity of federal institutions and the balance of the Canadian political system. But new objectives have appeared and even superseded the old ones. The interests at stake are somewhat prosaic. Two large bureaucratic empires are now facing each other over questions of taxation and spending authority. Two groups of politicians, federal and provincial, are in competition for the loyalty of the same group of people. But the whole process seems unreal because the voters are never presented with a clear-cut alternative that would let them show where their preference goes: federal or provincial. They are not given the kind of choice that would allow them to resolve the issue. Even the referendum offered only vague and hypothetical alternatives.

However, it is generally acknowledged that voters, whatever their political affinities, were quick to take advantage of this ambiguous situation. They saw in a confrontation that was ostensibly over the future of Canadian federalism a form of theatre which could not help but serve their collective interests. Although the provincial government's constitutional and fiscal offensive was completely stalled and political gains at the national level were proving illusory, it was impossible not to notice the slow decline of the English community within Quebec, a decline which resulted in a definite improvement of career opportunities for the French-speaking middle class. Naturally, there was reluctance to end a conflict that was thought, rightly or wrongly, to produce such happy results.

This static situation, pleasing just as much to the Parti Québécois as to the federal Liberals, diverted attention from the changes which were slowly taking place within Quebec society and which pointed to a dramatic transformation of the current political deadlock. Without politicians being quite aware of it, what seemed in the making was a mutation in the mental world which the Quiet Revolution had created and which subsequent events, such as the Parti Québécois' rise to power, had reinforced. Some intuitively felt that this was the end of an era in the history of Quebec and the beginning of a new one.

The first important figure to tie his political fate to the ground swell that seemed on the point of sweeping the province was Claude Ryan, the former publisher of the Montreal daily newspaper *Le Devoir*. In his campaign for the leadership of the provincial Liberal party and in the subsequent one which led to the federalist victory in the referendum on sovereignty-association, Ryan showed he was very much aware that a growing number of Quebecers had a view of the future very different from the one which current politics seemed to convey. He foresaw that the historical solidarity of French Canada would have to assume a new form and express itself in a manner which previous generations could never have imagined. Accordingly, his attacks on contemporary nationalism became more and more pressing, particularly on the type propounded by the Parti Québécois, which he considered an outmoded form of political action.

Of course, antinationalism was not a new phenomenon in Quebec. It had always been present as the inevitable counterweight to the occasionally excessive tendency of nationalism to conformity and conservatism. At various periods, it was the most usual form of opposition for those who opposed the isolationism of their compatriots and who wished for more intense participation in North American life. It is this tradition which Pierre Trudeau followed. However, there were no political risks attached to his antinationalism; on the contrary, he stood to profit from the very strength of nationalism in the sense that along with its spokesmen he dominated the political scene. Claude Ryan, on the other hand, staked everything on a frontal assault from within Quebec. He attacked nationalism as an ideology, as a representation of the world, and as a social project. He did this at the very moment when nationalism seemed most successful, when it had acquired status as the only legitimate representation of French national reality in Quebec.

At the beginning of the referendum campaign, the provincial Liberal party put forward a series of proposals which challenged the basic nationalist dogmas which had come to be almost automatically accepted by a majority of voters, including provincial civil servants and a large number of people who supported neither the Parti Québécois nor the idea of political independence. One of the reflex actions attacked most vigorously by Claude Ryan was the long-pursued drive to put as much distance between provincial and federal institutions as was compatible with sound economics, this in the interests of cultural security.

If one may speak of originality in this respect, here is where it lies: by abandoning the tone and style of a union negotiator whose principal, if not exclusive, concern is to reap as many benefits possible from a business whose general administration is left in the hands of other people, we have suggested that Quebec resolutely play the role of a major partner in a joint undertaking whose general well-being is just as important to him as the personal benefits he can derive from it. The Langlois Report has been criticized for not expressing a viewpoint which is narrowly and jealously that of Quebec. But this is precisely what constitutes its originality.[3]

Ryan also criticized the nationalist tendency to place national and cultural considerations ahead of everything else and to favour collective rights at the expense of individual ones. What he proposed was a complete reversal of this order of priorities, not only within Quebec where the French are in a majority but across Canada where they happen to be in a minority. This is a highly sensitive point bearing directly on collective anxiety about survival.

Formerly, everything that concerned collective life was expected to meet the requirements of a burdensome and rigid system of religious beliefs. Now it seems that this spirit has been transposed from religion to nationalism. In the eyes of certain people, cultural and linguistic differences explain everything, determine everything, must be present everywhere, and must constitute the obligatory basis for any political undertaking. However, we believe

3. Claude Ryan, "Le Rapport Langlois et l'avenir du fédéralisme canadien: notes pour un discours prononcé devant la Chambre de commerce de Montréal," 5 February, 1980 (author's translation).

that in a country such as Canada one must also take into account other extremely important considerations, particularly other values common to all citizens, the existence of vast and highly differentiated regions, as well as the fact that about 30 per cent of the country's population is made up of persons whose origins are neither French nor English. The Langlois Commission has insisted that the fundamental fact of linguistic and cultural duality be broadly recognized. But it has insisted on other considerations as well. Among all the elements which constitute Canadian reality, it has tried to distinguish and affirm certain common traits, particularly certain human rights which are more fundamental than the differences derived from language or culture.[4]

Even though these statements went directly against the nationalist rhetoric of the previous twenty years, popular reaction was positive. The broad support given the provincial Liberals after their dramatic about-face may be partly attributed to the interest and enthusiasm greeting a new party leader. However, the transformation of the parliamentary opposition was the most visible indication among many others that times had changed. In spite of their very favourable attitude towards René Lévesque's government, voters were unusually receptive to any critique of nationalism as well as to denunciations of the pro-independence movement. But this unpredictable shift of public opinion went far beyond the limited framework within which federalism and independence were being discussed. Not only did it affect the ideological content of nationalism but it concerned the relationships between groups and between individuals in Quebec's French society.

Before 1976, nationalism was one of many elements which helped determine social attitudes and influenced government decisions. After the election of the Parti Québécois in 1976, and as the PQ began implementing its cultural and linguistic

4. Ibid.

program, nationalism took on a new significance. Almost overnight, it became closely identified with a political party and with the various interest groups on which it depended to stay in power: the provincial bureaucracy, professionals, employees in cultural industries and services, the labour movement, intellectuals, and students. Under these circumstances, nationalism quickly became something to be either opposed or supported. Indeed, among those who were not sharing in the benefits accruing from the exercise of political power, it came to be perceived as an instrument of social control and of ideological conformity which certain privileged groups manipulated for their own purposes.

There is among certain segments of Quebec society a growing resistance to the idea of subordinating personal expectations to the collective goals identified with nationalism and with cultural and even ethnic solidarity. A substantial number of people feel excluded and marginalized by those who wield political power and those who benefit from it. Others are apprehensive about the cultural isolation which might result from a complete and overwhelming victory of nationalism.

While the Parti Québécois was implementing its language policies and preparing for the referendum, all these disparate elements naturally gravitated towards the provincial Liberal party which, until the arrival of Claude Ryan, had weakly allowed itself to drift into the wake of the nationalist movement. During the referendum campaign, however, these forces constituted only a circumstantial and temporary coalition; only later could there be a consolidation which might allow them to take power in the name of a new majority with a program and a philosophy distinct from that of the Parti Québécois and its allies.

For more than twenty years, nationalism had been the dominant ideology and had profoundly influenced the three parties that had wielded power during that period: the Liberals, the Union Nationale, and the Parti Québécois. The political energies which its presence generated speeded up the modernization of mentalities and institutions. The revival of nationalist sentiment helped overcome the fierce resistance of traditional elites to a reversal of government spending policies in favour of urban and industrial interests, at the expense of rural and agricultural ones.

The unprecedented progress achieved during this period of intense political activity did not benefit all classes and groups equally. New forms of discrimination emerged as the satisfaction of nationalist sentiment came to be a leading objective of government. Discriminatory treatment and preferential access to power gradually appeared and became more visible following the Parti Québécois' election victory of 1976. Because of its unusually high level of militancy, the party had a strong propensity to define its goals in relation to the social classes that had given it support; by the same token, it tended to discriminate against those groups who still believed in Canadian federalism and who wished to preserve existing links with the rest of the country.

The main group failing to establish satisfactory relations with the new government was made up of French businessmen and industrialists. The question of independence was obviously an important source of disagreement; business feared that a political break with the rest of the country might be followed in short order by an economic one. However, the real problem was elsewhere. A muted ideological struggle had developed between business leaders and government technocrats. Two modes of social organization were in conflict, one founded on economics and the other on political and cultural considerations. One side feared that the inconsiderate expansion of public services and a corresponding rise in tax levels might hinder economic growth; the other wanted to bring about a greater measure of social justice in the interests of stability and further progress.

It was during the referendum campaign that the animosity between businessmen and the Parti Québécois reached its highest point. The economic criticism of independence was such a powerful weapon in the hands of businessmen and federalists that the supporters of sovereignty-association regularly denounced it as blackmail and as the argument of fear. After the referendum defeat, Premier Lévesque described it as "this reflex of an old Quebec which we must accept," that is, the negative reflex which consists in equating independence with an economic gamble. Nevertheless, the economic arguments against the Parti Québécois acquired a great deal of credibility. The scorn and suspicion with which the party treated businessmen in general, particularly those who had regular contacts with their English-speaking counterparts, suggested that the party might not be able to tackle the economic problems resulting from independence.

Many other groups also came to dissociate themselves from the kind of nationalism projected by those who happened to be in power. The most remarkable dissidence was that displayed by women during the referendum campaign itself. Many of them were obviously housewives whom social isolation and economic dependence had rendered somewhat apprehensive of abrupt political change. Their conservatism, whose origin was largely occupational, was the target of much sarcasm on the part of certain leading personalities in the Parti Québécois. A large number of women were offended by this incomprehension and tactlessness.

Many working women also had reasons not to applaud the achievements associated with nationalism. Discrimination on the job market constituted the principal cause of their disaffection. Economic expansion, the rapid increase of public spending, and intergovernment rivalries had stimulated the growth of the first large French-speaking bureaucratic empires, such as the provincial public service and Hydro-Quebec. The factors which played against French-speaking executives and professionals in the large English-speaking corporations and in the federal service were exactly the same as those which hindered the advancement of women.

The larger the organization, the more recruitment tends to reflect the prejudices of the majority. Large corporations always seek to preserve the greatest homogeneity possible among their staff in order to ensure harmonious operations and eliminate possible sources of tensions and rivalries. Consequently, women have the same experience as ethnic minorities: they find it difficult to make headway in large corporations and in the public service and they generally do much better in small and medium-sized organizations.

In these circumstances, many women reject nationalist values, at least the current ones associated with the unprecedented expansion in the role of the state, with administrative centralization, and with bloated bureaucratic pyramids. Because of the discrimination they meet in the job market, especially at the management level, women will lean towards individualism and the kind of social system that favours it. Ethnic minorities will have the same reaction to the abuses perpetrated more or less consciously by the majority.

The referendum campaign also brought to light the dissatisfaction of many other groups. Elderly persons, pensioners, those in the least-paid and least-esteemed occupations, those whose chances of advancement are compromised by lack of education, all of them had their own reasons to reject sovereignty-association and contemporary nationalism. They could not help but be envious of the well-being and security granted to civil servants and to unionized workers and professionals, the very people who happen to be the most active supporters of nationalist policies. They could not help noticing by way of contrast their own insecurity and that of the great mass of nonunionized workers.

There are, in fact, strong popular suspicions regarding the two main constituents of the coalition that is keeping the Parti Québécois in power, the public service and the labour movement. Current inflationary pressures and economic problems are widely held to be caused by the excessive spending of governments, the low productivity of civil servants, and the exaggerated demands of organized labour. Voters who think this way tended to oppose the Parti Québécois government and its proposal for sovereignty-association, and most of them rallied behind the Liberals and federalism.

As was the case with housewives and women in traditional roles, Parti Québécois spokesmen encouraged disaffection. During the referendum campaign, public opinion polls consistently showed that the poorest and least-educated people tended to be federalists while the best-educated and most dynamic elements were mostly behind the government. This way of interpreting political trends was self-serving and it flattered nationalist vanity, but it was not shared by all. It intensified social division and further weakened the momentum of the nationalist movement.

If the poor and the uneducated acted the way they did, it was mainly because they felt excluded from the benefits of power, underrepresented and rejected by those groups who were most prominent in their support of the Parti Québécois. They felt marginalized by the arrogance of the public service and the selfishness of organized labour. In other words, there was a widespread feeling that the ruling political groups had broken with the ideal of equality and solidarity which had been the foundation of national survival. Consequently, the prospect of independence appeared a risky one for all those at the bottom of the social ladder. Distrust of nationalism rose sharply as a growing number of voters saw it as the instrument of privileged and powerful social groups.

The attack on nationalist values came from a variety of sources and was very prominent in the field of education. In Montreal, it was waged by militant Catholic parents who, beyond purely religious interests, sought to retain political control over the education given their children in the schools. In the course of the educational reform launched in the early 1960s, parents' rights had been severely curtailed in order to meet the needs of a modern industrial society for technical and managerial skills. School boards became mere agents of the government and of the bureaucracy. Meanwhile, teachers and their union organizations whittled away what was left of parental influence in school committees in order to gain as much professional control as possible over their jobs and their working conditions.

In 1977 Parti Québécois supporters and Catholics faced each other in the election of representatives to the Montreal Catholic School Commission. Each group had its own program, one favouring the socialization of educational goals while the other insisted on individual and family values. Catholics handily won the election, in which the level of popular participation was scandalously low. It was a victory that many considered equivocal.

The election demonstrated one of the glaring weaknesses of the Parti Québécois and of the nationalist movement: their inability to inspire their supporters and encourage their participation in projects whose impact is purely local or sectorial. A school board contest, where government policies on education are being challenged by part of the local population, does not seem important enough to arouse the interest of party supporters. They are attracted only to comprehensive and collective projects and their ideological commitment to a cause does not necessarily translate into action and participation.

Since 1976 there has been a noticeable institutional polarization within Quebec. To all intents and purposes, the provincial government dominates the political scene. Since it took power in 1976, the Parti Québécois government has concentrated its efforts on the achievement of national identity. The fact that this goal coincides with political trends of the last twenty years provides it with a very progressive and modern image. Yet centralization has generated considerable tensions with local institutions such as municipalities, school boards, and hospital administrations, as well as with private enterprise. These have continued to be concerned with local and sectorial issues which very often come into conflict with the broad social preoccupations of the provincial government. Unavoidably, they have acquired a very conservative reputation in a political context where the provincial government has acted as the promoter of social justice and of the common good.

Of course, each period has its own definition of what is progressive and what is reactionary. Towards the end of the Duplessis régime and at the beginning of the Quiet Revolution, nationalism was seen as an impediment to progress because it encouraged withdrawal into an archaic society with no future. Later, nationalism acquired a totally different significance when it became associated with modernization, the expansion of French cultural and economic territory, and the consolidation of national identity. Its image was completely rehabilitated in the minds of the majority because it corresponded exactly to the general idea of progress and of the common good.

With the adoption of the government's language legislation and with the prospect of a referendum on sovereignty-association, nationalist agitation intensified. But as the collective will came to be expressed increasingly in political terms, certain dissident and centrifugal forces began to make themselves felt. A reaction appeared from the very moment when the obsession with nationalism started to infiltrate every activity and to influence every decision. An increasing number of people could be heard in various types of organizations, such as the labour unions or in the feminist movement, expressing the wish that the so-called *question nationale* be resolved as quickly as possible so proper attention could be given to more concrete problems arising out of everyday activities. This constituted a definite cooling of the former fervour.

Quebec nationalists attribute a great deal of importance to political action. But their expectations have not all been realized and this has given rise to a certain disenchantment with that particular form of social involvement. René Lévesque has repeatedly insisted on his belief that politics was the most noble and useful career that one could pursue. Although this view of political leadership is shared by most people in Quebec, it subtly disparages the more modest personal objectives of private life. It establishes a hierarchy of values which in the end can become oppressive. Accordingly, in the manner of a pendulum inevitably swinging in the opposite direction, weariness with collective goals and a thirst for personal achievement began to affect the political scene. There appeared a genuine desire to cast off the paralysing influence of mass politics.

French-speaking voters happened to be in an unusual state of receptiveness when Claude Ryan proposed his antinationalist program to the provincial Liberal party in 1978. An inclination towards regimentation and the excesses of political confrontations had dimmed the virtue of nationalist causes and reversed the politicization of national sentiment. French Quebec seemed on the point of acceding to a new vision of social reality. The ideas which had been guiding political action for twenty years or so were losing their relevance. New ones, still largely undefined, were now taking shape.

However, the process of substitution and of transformation was not solely the product of a psychological weariness with a constant rehearsal of the same basic themes and the same arguments. New facts, with a well-defined and easily verifiable impact, were also exerting an irresistible influence on popular perceptions of government's role in society, on business and the economy, on the contents of French culture, and on North American continentalism. The Liberals were the first to take note and adapt themselves to the new political situation. The Parti Québécois, bogged down in the exercise of power, was slower to react; but it eventually did adjust while avoiding any move that might unduly alarm militant nationalist elements in its ranks.

The most important of the new facts to emerge towards the end of the 1970s was the abrupt termination of the rapid and steady expansion which public services had experienced since 1960.

Earlier, the government of Maurice Duplessis had been extremely timid in its borrowing and parsimonious in its spending. When Jean Lesage came to power in 1960, therefore, the government enjoyed an unusually wide margin of credit and eagerly made use of it. The general economic situation encouraged high and even reckless spending: the first manifestations of inflation appearing at that time swelled public revenues and created the illusion that the province's financial resources were inexhaustible. It was then that public services started to expand almost uncontrollably, but in a way that gave satisfaction to everyone.

The administration of the welfare state was taken over by French-speaking professionals who, for the first time, were feeling the thrill and exaltation of bureaucratic power. This elite, which was coming out of universities in constantly growing numbers, automatically assumed a new role on behalf of the population: to ensure its cultural and material well-being by making use of all the powers of the state. It was a moral responsibility that helped revive the self-esteem of the French middle class, which had been severely undercut by its long and systematic exclusion from the management of large Canadian corporations.

After a decade of growth, however, the weight of bureaucracy made itself felt. Inflationary pressures, which had first encouraged a high level of public spending, now pushed costs upwards, causing them to outstrip the value of the services that were being offered to the population. Budget controls became increasingly severe, but this was hardly sufficient. It became necessary in the last resort to imitate other governments and to impose strict limits on the growth of the public service. In Quebec this policy had unusual consequences.

Because professionals and technocrats in key jobs are still relatively young, it will be some time before interesting government jobs become available once again in adequate numbers for the graduates of colleges and universities. Most of them will have to resign themselves to careers outside the public service, which for almost twenty years has provided the principal professional outlet for the educated middle class. Consequently, the ideological attitudes favouring public service careers and social control will have to be phased out. As a replacement, there will have to be what one might call new occupational mentalities.

The prolonged freeze on government jobs means that the public service will lose a considerable part of its political influence and that it can no longer be considered one of the dynamic elements of Quebec society. One of the main supports of nationalism, and one of the bodies which have contributed most effectively to its ideological consolidation, has been neutralized by current economic trends as well as by the parallel transformation of general social attitudes, particularly those of the middle class itself.

Another new development, the rapid francization of the provincial economy, offers wide opportunities to a large number of young university graduates whom the public service can no longer absorb. It springs from the political will of the French majority in Quebec to put an end to the preeminence of the English language in business and to the near-monopoly of English-speaking people in management jobs in large corporations with sizeable operations in the province. Although corporate resistance has been strong, francization is everywhere perceived as an inevitable and almost natural process which provincial authorities have only encouraged.

Nonetheless, in a broader context it is clear that the displacement of economic decision centres from Montreal towards Toronto and other points west has made francization immeasurably easier and less traumatic politically. This migration, which corresponds to an earlier and similar movement in the United States, has created a vacuum which French-speaking businessmen and professionals have tried to fill. Moreover, the regionalization of the Canadian economy—its balkanization, as it is described by the heads of large Canadian corporations who fear the administrative and political fragmentation of the country—offers French Canada new opportunities for expansion. The economic importance of the French language will be much greater in a regionalized context than in a situation of complete integration into Canadian life.

Indeed, French society in Quebec seems better disposed than it ever was to accept the risks involved in a precarious equilibrium between unproductive isolation and assimilation. Similarly, there is a certain relaxation of the collective solidarity forged during the period of transformation and tension which began in 1960 and during which the abolition of all political and cultural risk had become a veritable obsession. The return to individualism, especially in the economic realm, is contributing to a revival of creative activity inasmuch as individuals are much more daring and innovative than whole communities.

Another important consideration in the present situation is the imbalance between the productivity of the Quebec economy and the expansion of the tertiary sector, that is, the services produced by professionals. The disproportion, which reflects low production levels, encourages high taxation of that part of the population which is most productive and prosperous. But at the same time, the poorest and least educated are demoralized and rendered dependent in a way that nationalists will attribute to the "system" or to capitalist exploitation.

Even before all these problems—the job freeze in the public service, the francization of the economy, and the overdevelopment of public services—could attract the attention of politicians and of the public, they had already produced unconscious modifications in personal expectations. The wave resulting from the cumulative impact of individual judgments has acquired such a force that Quebec might be said to be in the middle of an ideological mutation such as has periodically occurred throughout its history.

The achievement of a basic nationalist objective, the modernization of mentalities and institutions, has caused the decline of the very things nationalist sentiment depended on for its survival: group solidarity, egalitarianism, and social cohesiveness. These values, which were an undeniable source of progress for twenty years, suddenly became constraining for a growing number of individuals who were taking stock of a promising new situation and who aspired to a greater measure of personal independence and initiative. It was a psychological transformation in line with the attitudes that already prevailed in the rest of North America.

Already, it is apparent that private enterprise and business will emerge as the most dynamic sector of French society in Quebec, the one whose achievements will determine future prospects. It will have an impact as great as the establishment of a large bureaucratic apparatus has had on the period which is now coming to a close. Public servants and politicians will necessarily have to establish a close relationship with those who are pursuing careers in private business and they will have to provide social and political support by means of new policies adapted to the needs of French businessmen and to the competitive situation they will be facing.

In the end, nationalism is destined to decline as a political movement. It can no longer be expected to dominate public debates as it has now done for more than twenty years. Timelier and more concrete concerns will be taking its place.

New Perspectives

An unmistakable indication of the imminent reversal of political values in Quebec is—paradoxically—the anxiety which the English presence continues to inspire among nationalist elements in spite of the immense progress of French in the last generation. Even though the use of English is becoming more circumscribed, a large number of people still perceive it as a threat to French survival, as if any accommodation between the two would inevitably work to the detriment of the French language.

This pessimistic view has inspired nationalists in politics and in the public service to oppose categorically the recognition of collective or group rights for the English-speaking minority. As far as they are concerned, only French exclusiveness and monopoly of public communications can safeguard the future of their language. They show an irreducible opposition to everything English. As a form of nationalism it is distinct from that based on an eye for an eye, but sometimes coexists with it. English culture, whether Canadian or American, clearly assumes a subversive character.

Such anxiety, whose strange and obsessive quality foreshadows an abrupt social mutation, resembles the militant anticommunism which prevailed under Maurice Duplessis. In the immediate postwar period, urban and industrial pressures weighed heavily on a society which was desperately clinging to traditional rural values for the sake of security. The future was viewed with a great deal of apprehension. In order to ward off undesirable social changes and to underscore their dangerous nature, the search was on for agents of subversion.

Attacks on communism served to dramatize the defence of institutions and social structures which at the time were thought to be vital. Communism arose out of the brutality of the urban and industrial experience of the nineteenth century in Europe and was not really pertinent to Quebec, but it nonetheless offered a plausible and convincing target for most people. Authorities found it was very easy to rally the population to this kind of crusade as most Western countries were already caught up in the ideological struggle with the Soviet Union known as the Cold War.

It was also at that very moment that the whole of American society was launched on a veritable witch-hunt designed to eliminate socialists and communist sympathizers from every post in the public service, the labour movement, and industries such as communications, information, and entertainment. This modern Inquisition, personified by Senator Joseph McCarthy and conducted by the Senate Committee on Un-American Activities, abruptly came to an end in the early 1960s just as the revolt of the black ghettos in large American cities and the radical student movement began to make headlines everywhere. In the United States, as in Quebec, anticommunism was a form of resistance to changes of mentality which were occurring unconsciously and which would soon bring about sweeping social changes.

In Quebec, the obsessive anticommunism of the 1950s constituted a last psychological rampart against the advent of the Quiet Revolution and the welfare state. The cultural anxiety triggered by the visible presence of English-language institutions in Montreal plays an analogous role. The will displayed by many intellectuals in government and politics to limit as much as possible the influence of English-language institutions aims at creating a climate unfavourable to changes in social attitudes. The resistance is centred on the desire to forestall a new revolution which might threaten the status of intellectuals as a special social group with a definite place in the history of Quebec. If the struggle generates so much anxiety, it is that there may be subconscious doubts about its usefulness.

The threat which the English presence in Quebec represents can hardly be considered as solely linguistic or demographic. The English community, with its institutions and its economic power, is directly identified with the liberal society of North America and represents, as it were, the enemy within. Its presence is worrisome precisely because a majority of French-speaking people in Quebec are eager to integrate into North American society and to accept its ideological foundations. It is thought that curbing the influence of the English community will arrest trends which are felt to be undesirable and even dangerous for French Quebec.

The decline of nationalism in Quebec points to the day when the man of action rather than the man of thought will impose his values and his outlook on the majority. The prestige and influence of intellectuals and of educated people in general will be somewhat curtailed. It would be very surprising, for example, if there were a repetition of the present situation whereby the premier of the province and the leader of the opposition in the National Assembly are both recruited from journalism. Their professional role was to explain the great political events of the day, to offer a critique of collective goals, and to shape popular thinking on a wide variety of issues. The importance attributed in French Quebec to these activities naturally attracted René Lévesque and Claude Ryan to this form of power and later propelled them into politics.

Journalists and intellectuals play a very different role in English Canada and in the rest of North America. Current trends in Quebec are leading to a painful social setback for a whole category of persons who have historically assumed the status almost of a distinct social class and who have traditionally exercised normative functions in French society. It is this eventuality that the bulk of the nationalist movement is seeking to avert.

Just as the communist menace was once conjured up in order to do away with the prospect of a social-democratic society which was contemplated with a great deal of concern, the English menace represents the thin edge of liberalism and particularly of pluralism, gradually invading a society which seeks to remain homogeneous and egalitarian and where the old minority reflexes are still very strong. It is not that English-speaking people are scapegoats for others' offences. What we have is an ill-considered search for a point of attack against those values which seem the most unfavourable and the most threatening to the old order.

This transformation of Quebec society, however, has been in progress for quite some time already. The most eloquent and conclusive sign of the changes now under way in social attitudes has been the steady growth of the charismatic movement, which has almost revolutionized the nature of religious sentiment in Quebec over the last ten years. Its attitudes conform very closely to the individualism which is asserting itself vigorously in the realm of politics as well as in those of business and work.

Because of its evangelical character and the personal faith it promotes, the charismatic movement in the Catholic Church is quite close to the spirit of Protestantism. The type of Catholicism which predominated in Quebec until 1960 exhibited many traits which have now largely disappeared: domination by a clergy tending to be authoritarian, jealous, sometimes parasitic, and inimical to personal thought, which it stifled under the crushing weight of dogma and doctrine. Together with individualism, which it encourages and fosters, the charismatic movement stands for liberation from institutional and ideological constraints as well as accession to an unaccustomed form of freedom whose effects are bound to be felt in many areas other than religion.

Nevertheless, the real revolution worked by the charismatic movement has been to detach religion and religious sentiment from their close association with national survival. Relieved of the historical burden imposed upon it towards the middle of the nineteenth century, religious faith has turned away from the social and civic character it then exhibited to become more personal and mystical. By all accounts, the quality of religious life throughout the Church in Quebec improved immeasurably as it came to depend on individuals rather than on the collectivity and on groups. Like the abrupt drop in the birth rate that took place in the late 1950s, this development is the forerunner of a wrenching but liberating break with the past and with age-old ways of being.

The desire to be free from the pressure of groups and of the collectivity does not manifest itself solely in the field of religion. There is a widespread desire for self-fulfilment in many other areas. Just as members of the Church no longer want the clergy to have sole responsibility for determining their faith and their conduct, a growing number of people will resist having their goals and expectations formulated in their name by others, whether culturally, socially, or politically. It is as if the very ideals of autonomy and independence that nationalism had long demanded on behalf of the collectivity had progressively been taken over by individuals that are part of it. Eventually, the internal equilibrium of Quebec society is bound to be profoundly modified.

As suggested by the Créditiste revolt of the early 1960s, Quebec has come to the end of a historical period which began in the first part of the nineteenth century and during which intellectuals and educated people provided an essential form of social and political leadership. The mission which they took upon themselves also favoured a recourse to paternalism and it justified the existence of an elitist and hierarchical society, in spite of the egalitarian yearnings expressed everywhere.

The practical consequences of this new state of affairs can be readily anticipated. It is more than likely that there will be readjustments in fiscal policies, which in the past fifteen years or so have been leaning heavily in the direction of egalitarianism. There will no doubt be moves to offer greater incentives for personal effort and initiative. By the same token, the government will not be so eager to ensure the economic security of individuals and will be disposed to cut the budgets allocated to the pursuit of the welfare state. In other words, the resources of the community will be made to serve the ends of economic productivity rather than those of social justice.

These readjustments, which the Parti Québécois for obvious electoral considerations will not reject, are already being put into effect at the federal level, in the other provinces, and in the United States. Inflationary pressures coupled with economic stagnation everywhere require drastic changes in fiscal policies. In spite of its somewhat unique situation, Quebec remains attuned to trends across the continent and is proceeding to bring about the same policy reversals.

The shift away from social democracy towards economic liberalism is bound to transform the coalition which took power in 1976 with the election of the Parti Québécois. It can be expected that politicians, technocrats, and professionals in the public service will gradually draw closer to businessmen and to those who wield power in the private sector. The so-called favourable prejudice which the party claims to feel towards the labour movement, the moderate left, and intellectuals in general will likely give way to indifference, if not to outright suspicion. Indeed, the party itself could lead the way towards a new conservatism in spite of the ideological rigidity displayed by a substantial proportion of its leaders and organizers. But one should not necessarily conclude that the move is inspired by opportunism and cynicism.

Lionel Groulx's personal experience in the political context of the first half of the twentieth century might confirm his contention that "any liberating movement proceeds from thinkers to the crowd." Even today, mostly on the left, there are people who believe that an aggressive minority can push social development in a predetermined direction. However, the fragility of this particular notion is obvious from the very efforts of left-wing political groups in Quebec to seek approval by invoking popular roots which are more or less illusory if not entirely fictitious.

It would be more appropriate today to describe politicians as unconscious instruments of the popular will, or to say that the longevity of any politician derives from his ability to personify the popular will rather than from his aptitude for leading it. These considerations could apply equally well to thinkers and intellectuals. Those who persist in exercising the historical mission of leadership and social control which had once been attributed to them will find their appeal today limited to small militant groups and clans. The current view is that intellectuals should provide their contemporaries with some kind of a mirror, an echo of their feelings and of their expectations. This is why intellectual life is gradually shifting towards more personal and individual activities instead of being bound up in the quest for some form of national identity. Literary and artistic production in Quebec will reflect this change.

Already it is possible to note a definite depreciation of nationalist ideals, going beyond the unavoidable weariness of the population with the endless debates over constitutional options and referendum choices. There is a growing skepticism among rank-and-file labour, as a result of the excessive use of nationalist symbols by the Confederation of National Trade Unions in its raiding ventures against affiliates of the Quebec Federation of Labour, and by the latter in its campaign for a greater measure of autonomy from the Canadian Labour Congress and from international unions.

The trivialization of nationalist symbols was also brought on by the marketing of consumer goods, which in Quebec relied extensively on advertising based on themes such as heritage, tradition, and collective identity. The use of concepts related to politics began towards the end of the 1960s in the marketing of a broad range of products including beer. After the election of the Parti Québécois in 1976, it became obvious that the returns from this type of advertising were falling off very rapidly. But the fact that consumers had become somewhat jaded does not explain completely what happened then. Nor does the imminent satisfaction of nationalist goals as a result of the Parti Québécois' election.

The problem was that advertising could no longer address itself to a homogenized mass of consumers; it had to adjust to a segmented market and to a highly differentiated public. The erosion of family life, steady improvements in the standard of living, and more personal conceptions of individual activities and consumption had contributed in altering public attitudes and responses to advertising messages. That in itself was an important social transformation.

It would not be surprising, in this situation, to discover that the feelings of anxiety generated by the presence of English institutions have a tendency to recede, and that this reduces the political impact of the ethnic and linguistic confrontations that Quebec has experienced since the end of the 1960s. This is to say that apprehension over the French language's chances of survival in North America will gradually become nonpolitical, just as nationalism seems to be doing, and will tend to invade the realm of interpersonal relations, particularly at work. Whatever frictions persist will be interpersonal rather than between language groups.

It would be a perfectly normal reaction for the English-speaking community to express some kind of relief at the decline of nationalist sentiment. When tensions were at their height, towards 1977, nationalist attacks threatened its cultural vitality and its economic strength as government legislation began to require corporate francization and the enrolment in French schools of children of immigrants and of English-speaking people from other parts of Canada. However, the problems of the English community in Montreal, which began long before nationalism appeared on the scene, will not necessarily be resolved by a return to liberal values and the abandonment of coercive cultural planning by government authorities. English-speaking people will face stiff competition on the job, particularly from the French middle class. It will be most intense at the management level in those sections of large Canadian corporations that deal with the Quebec market. It is because of all the transformations that have taken place since 1960 that this competition becomes possible.

During the period spanning the 1960s and the 1970s, French society managed to realize a form of unity to which its elites have long aspired but which had always eluded them. In the cultural state of siege that seems an almost permanent feature of life in Quebec, unity has been conceived of primarily in ideological terms. For example, towards the end of the last century, there was the indissoluble trinity of *la foi, la langue, la race*—faith, language, race. As a sort of slogan, it succinctly described the nature of the bonds which were meant to ensure the solidarity as well as the homogeneity of that society.

Unfortunately, the extremely restrictive way in which the dominant ideology was formulated served only to marginalize all those who insisted on living in a more open society and who pursued intellectual activities other than perpetuating a culture capable of surviving only in total isolation. The principal shortcoming of that ideology, which acquired a great deal of prominence early in the twentieth century as a defence against Anglo-Canadian capitalism, was that it diverted attention from a vital consideration: the importance of economic activities and the influence they ultimately exert on the organization of society and on political thinking itself.

The most visible and profound divisions made their appearance during the regime of Maurice Duplessis, after the Second World War and just as Quebec was about to embark on a process of modernization and development without parallel in its history. There was at that time a fundamental opposition between the rural and the urban populations, between agriculture and industry, between the whole of the province and Montreal, between the world of culture and that of the economy, between those who were inward-looking and those who were interested in the outside world and yearned for new ideas. Yet, contrary to what had happened in earlier times, no person or institution was powerful enough to paste over the gaping social cracks that stood in the way of unity and concerted action. Authorities, both civil and religious, had to resign themselves to the existence of a second French society beyond the traditional bounds of French power.

An important result of this compromise, inspired as much by helplessness as by wisdom, was that it allowed opponents of the regime to escape persecution by taking refuge in the numerous sanctuaries which the duality of French society afforded. At that time, the business world in Montreal offered political and material security. In addition, the institutions of the English community, particularly the universities, offered some protection in spite of their submissive and deferential attitudes to authority. However, it was within the federal public service that resistance was fiercest, and particularly in Radio-Canada, which then provided the type of intellectual leadership that helped Quebec focus on more contemporary values.

The magnitude of the changes that have taken place since the times of Duplessis can be measured by Radio-Canada's relations with federal power and French Quebec today. According to numerous spokesmen in the federal government and the Quebec Liberal caucus in the House of Commons, Radio-Canada personnel are actively promoting, in news broadcasts and public-affairs programs, nationalistic ideas favourable to Quebec independence, contrary to the mandate which the corporation was given by Parliament to promote national unity. These complaints have been voiced for years but little has been done. The situation demonstrates the impossibility for the federal government of controlling the internal operations of an institution which it created and which it is funding. It shows the extent to which political relationships have been altered during this long period of nationalist tension.

The extent to which public opinion has polarized between the rival concepts of federalism and independence has tended to obscure the real nature of the changes that have taken place in Quebec. The marginality which the Duplessis regime used to enforce on its opponents has given way to ideological pluralism and hence to a greater degree of tolerance, this in spite of the highly emotional character of political debates in Quebec. Similarly, the manner in which opponents of the regime used to reject traditional society and its institutions has itself given way to a desire for participation and integration which rules out destructive confrontations. The relative serenity with which the Liberals accepted their defeat in both the 1976 and 1981 provincial elections, and the Parti Québécois its loss of the referendum on sovereignty-association in 1980, indicates that there is now a broad acceptance of the rules of politics which hardly existed twenty years earlier.

Since the beginning of the Quiet Revolution there has been a transfer of popular allegiance towards provincial institutions to the detriment of federal ones. Although nationalism has played an important role in this movement, its spirit remains rooted in regionalism. It is in this manner that the takeover of Radio-Canada has been accomplished, under the cover of separatist subversion as it were. A comparable transformation has also taken place in that part of the federal service located in Quebec. Just as in the provincial service, the trend has been towards French exclusiveness at the expense of Montreal's English community, which has been deprived of its traditional participation in the management of public affairs. In this respect, federal authorities have been just as unsuccessful in Quebec as in other provinces with their policies of bilingualism and biculturalism.

It is interesting in this regard to recall the statements that Prime Minister Trudeau used to make, before the referendum, on the possible advent of separatism. People would recognize it, he said, by the French population's desertion of federal institutions and their lack of interest in them. But there was neither desertion nor separation. What happened was a progressive regional takeover of federal institutions in Quebec territory. This was an eventuality that no one had foreseen. The prime minister's analysis of the situation, centred on current political confrontations, rapidly became obsolete. The same thing happened to the charges of treason which ultranationalists regularly levelled at the prime minister and his associates: they are part of an ideological world which is rapidly receding into the past.

The antinationalism of Pierre Trudeau and of his contemporaries has its roots in the struggle which progressive elements waged against the Duplessis regime during the 1950s, a struggle which eventually brought on the Quiet Revolution. To the Union Nationale's rural, authoritarian, and isolationist ideology, they opposed an open-minded attitude to change. Freedom and progress were identified with the federal government, and provincialism and regionalism were denounced as retrograde. The idea underlying this particular vision of politics is that large organizations are more efficient and better equipped to ensure progress and social equilibrium, and to meet the needs of the individual. But time and experience have shown that this assumption is not necessarily correct, whether for a country or for a corporate organization.

Because of the excessive polarization to which it has given rise, Pierre Trudeau's antinationalism has become a regressive element in Quebec politics, and has delayed reexamination of the Parti Québécois' ideology. His views originate in the fragmented and isolationist society of the 1950s and have not changed since then. They have very little to do with the unified and pluralistic society that is emerging today. While the provincial Liberal party under Claude Ryan has psychologically entered a new political era, and while the Parti Québécois is also trying to adapt itself to new circumstances, the Liberal Party of Canada and its leader are still clinging to modes of thought and to rallying points that have lost a great deal of their validity.

The political struggle which federal authorities have been waging almost since the beginning of the Quiet Revolution centres on the merits of a large political system such as Canada's and the destructive effects of regionalism on the national economy. Ottawa's constitutional policy, just as Premier Lévesque's plans for independence, raises the crucial question as to what type of boundaries will satisfy French-speaking Quebecers; or, expressed another way, how much of an opening they want on the outside world. The two orders of government involved with the issue would like the question answered in a way that will maximize their own power and authority, which it would be naïve to identify with the public good.

After the referendum of May 1980, Prime Minister Trudeau took advantage of the euphoria created by the federalist victory to attack a serious problem of the Canadian economy, one that had lately grown more acute. This was the gradual balkanization of the national economy, mainly under the impact of provincial laws and regulations. The transfer from the British to the Canadian Parliament of authority over the constitution was to be the occasion for a more precise definition of the nature and the extent of the powers of the central government. The leading objective would be to restore the integrity of the Canadian market for goods and services and to eliminate all existing obstacles to the free circulation of persons and capital. Examples of restrictions to be done away with are the obligation to reinvest a fixed proportion of insurance premiums in the province where they were collected and the preferential treatment given by most governments in their purchasing policies to local manpower, goods, and services.

This constitutional reform tends towards the abolition of the barriers which the Quebec government had been setting up for more than twenty years. The province's concept of constitutional equilibrium was formulated by Claude Morin, minister for intergovernmental affairs in René Lévesque's cabinet and previously deputy minister of the same department under four successive premiers. In his view, the jurisdiction attributed to each order of government was to be as airtight as possible and supported by exclusive taxation powers. Inevitable administrative overlaps were to be resolved by formal agreements between Ottawa and Quebec, somewhat in the form of a peace treaty. Such was the official way of defending French cultural interests before the notion of political independence upset all attempts at compromise and accommodation.

However, independently of government action, new barriers have been cropping up according to the development of each region and of each community in the country. The most important ones result from the movement of the top management and of the headquarters of large Canadian corporations from Montreal to Toronto and other points west. This migration corresponds to a similar one in the United States but happens to be reinforced by the desire to avoid making any concessions to French Quebec.

Hundreds of firms have been affected by this type of decision, and what remains of their Quebec operations invariably becomes French. The new managers will have a very strong tendency to assert their independence from the head office outside the province. Their interests will be concentrated on the market they serve and within which their careers unfold. Their loyalty will go to the French economy of Quebec and to their French colleagues rather than to their superiors who belong to the English economy of Canada. Inevitably, Quebec will develop into a relatively autonomous growth centre and its contacts with the outside will therefore lose the integrated and organic character they once had.

Whether federal authorities are successful or not in their attempts to do away with the legal and commercial barriers that the provinces have set up between themselves is of only relative importance for Quebec. These barriers, or those which are of a constitutional order, will play only a secondary role in the development of the country compared to future divisions based on the conjunction of economic and linguistic factors. The future of federalism will depend to a very large extent on its ability to handle the unexpected turn taken by the historical rivalry between French and English.

In this perspective, the assumptions behind Prime Minister Trudeau's constitutional proposals seem somewhat anachronistic and out of touch. The political order which he seeks to reestablish has been irretrievably left behind by the changes that have overtaken the country. Ever since Confederation, every administration in Ottawa has promoted industrial concentration and regional specialization as the foundation of Canadian unity and prosperity. However, for some years already, the provinces have been protesting against the economic vocations imposed upon them by the central government. This movement is particularly strong in the West, where accelerated industrialization is expected to do away with the personal and social constraints resulting from heavy dependence on agriculture and natural resources. And beyond federal policies, the West is challenging the preeminence of the central provinces, which have been the main beneficiaries of the economic and industrial strategy of the federal government.

Concurrently with these tensions, which are perfectly normal in such a diverse and thinly settled country as Canada, there is a deterioration in the equilibrium of the federal system. The pressures which originate from Quebec make it impossible to return to the old organizational principles of economic concentration and specialization. Quebec's recent accession to social unity, its acceptance of individualism, and the growth of a new entrepreneurial spirit in the province have given it an unprecedented concern with economic expansion. As a result French Quebec no longer interacts with Canada in the way it used to. There is a totally new situation.

In 1974 Robert Bourassa's government introduced legislation providing active and official support for the conversion of large corporations to the use of the French language. Until that time, the Canadian economy had exhibited a great unity of language, and hence of spirit; this ensured the homogeneity of the main decision centres responsible for planning and management from coast to coast. However, the situation could not remain as it was once the French language began to assert itself more vigorously. From the moment it spread beyond the social and political realms into that of the economy, which the English community in Montreal had always considered its own preserve, English Canada was cut into two unequal parts, the Maritime provinces to the east and Ontario, the Prairies, and British Columbia to the west.

The break in Canada's economic continuity from east to west contributed to the rise in regional sentiment everywhere and it heightened resistance to the centralizing policies of the federal government. The steady increase of energy prices reinforced these trends as some provinces sought to retain for themselves the benefits accruing from their resources instead of considering them as national assets. Thus the crisis arising out of this situation concerns mounting difficulties in mapping out workable compromises on economic policy and, specifically, the federal government's inability to exercise the leadership conferred upon it by the constitution.

During the nineteenth century, Montreal had been the heart of a huge commercial empire stretching from the Atlantic to the Pacific. The English community was then extremely powerful. But the city was bound to become predominantly French once the country's economic centre of gravity began moving westward, a process which got under way as early as the turn of the century but which did not become a political issue until much later. It was obvious that, with the decline of Montreal and its transformation into a regional rather than a national centre, it would become necessary for the business establishment to reflect the city's cultural character more closely than in the past, that it would have to make serious concessions to the French majority. Nationalists saw this as a process of decolonization and liberation. But it is in fact part of a process of maturation whose effects are being felt not only in Quebec but with a disconcerting force in the rest of Canada as well.

Federal authority was seriously weakened following French Quebec's awakening to economic realities. It had been sustained until then by Ontario's and Quebec's shared interest in maintaining the rest of the country in a state of economic dependence, or of semicolonialism as the other provinces would have it. Because Quebec was then divided into a rural society fearful of change and an urban one eager for modernization, it could hardly do more than play the part of a passive and silent partner in the political cartel that was Canada. However, the thorny issue of power-sharing between French and English, between Quebec and Ontario, came to the fore as the country's economic centre shifted westward and as business in Montreal acquired more of a French look. The practical impossibility of arriving at a solution which satisfied everyone put an end to the historic unity of central Canada, to its hegemony over the rest of the country, and to the unchallenged supremacy of federal authority.

The Canadian business establishment sealed the fate of Pierre Trudeau's brand of federalism by refusing to integrate French-speaking persons in the upper reaches of management and in head-office operations. In the absence of a viable understanding between Quebec and Ontario, the other provinces acquired a freedom of action and a corresponding independence which can nullify traditional policies and existing constitutional arrangements. By the same token, the Montreal-based economic empire which thrived from the end of the eighteenth century to the beginning of the twentieth practically ceased to exist. What must be resolved are the problems of reaching a new agreement between the constituent parts of the country. A new internal equilibrium must be found.

According to nationalists, hostility towards everything French explains English refusal to share economic power. It is true that English exclusivism is a historical fact, one to which Lord Durham paid a great deal of attention in his report to imperial authorities on the Rebellion of 1837 in Lower Canada. Nevertheless, there were periods when fruitful political compromises were arrived at, which avoided the paralysis of government institutions and the deterioration of the economy. The ones negotiated by Louis-Hippolyte Lafontaine in the 1840s and by George-Etienne Cartier at the time of Confederation, while hardly meeting current requirements, conformed to their contemporaries' assessment of their society's strengths and weaknesses. But in the present situation, it has been impossible to resolve the problem of economic power-sharing, in spite of the disastrous consequences that could result from failure. One must look beyond animosity and prejudice for an explanation.

Quebec's transformation into the odd man out of the federal system occurred while Canadian business was entering a period of rigidity and was encountering great difficulties in adapting to unsettled economic circumstances. In a manner parallel to that of government, private enterprise was becoming more bureaucratic and technocratic in its operations. The influence which a single individual can wield, even in the case of top-level executives, has become increasingly restricted by the almost insurmountable inertia of the organization to which he belongs. The organization is incapable of achieving what its members would seek individually.

It is in connection with the Quebec problem that the effects of this transformation are the most revealing. Unfortunately, the political impact of these changes in Canadian business have been obscured by French nationalism's quickness to take offence and its tendency to view differences with the English population of the country as irreconcilable. Thus, when companies such as Sun Life and Canadian Industries Limited announced they were moving their head offices from Montreal to Toronto, public opinion in Quebec did not dwell at all on the real significance of the reasons invoked. Being sensitive mostly to intimidation and insults, it paid little attention to what English-speaking businessmen were actually saying.

When Sun Life and CIL claim that the political situation in Quebec hinders recruitment of executives for their head offices in Montreal, these two companies are simply saying that the people who are pursuing careers in large Canadian corporations are afraid of culture shock and will accept only a familiar social environment which causes no personal problems. The lack of mobility attributed to members of the French-speaking middle class who are reluctant to accept jobs in the national capital or anywhere outside Quebec also exists among their English-speaking counterparts. The spirit of risk and adventure which businessmen once claimed for themselves is no longer there. The bureaucratic obsession with security and comfort is what predominates. It is thought preferable to retreat to Toronto rather than deal squarely with the problems arising in Montreal. There is no interest in arriving at some form of compromise with the French majority that might destroy the homogeneous character of the head office and upset corporate policies.

The same attitudes are reflected in the specific area of language. The argument has often been made, in order to avoid making any concessions to French, that English is the international language of business and science and hence that head-office operations must absolutely and exclusively be conducted in that language. What this expresses is a desire to shut oneself into a closed world free from external pressures. The one-dimensional culture in which Canadian business is taking refuge reveals a certain apprehension at the prospect of change and an unconscious desire to arrest the course of time. The addiction to routine, the quest for short-term profits, the absence of research and planning, rigidity in the face of social transformations, all these have become characteristic of big business in Canada.

However, conditions in Canada can hardly be dissociated from the broad North American context, where a somewhat typical problem is that of the automobile industry. The automakers' lack of responsiveness to the energy crisis has caused it to be overwhelmed by Japanese and European competition. American lack of business initiative translates into a declining interest in the technological research in industry, concentration on the most easily marketable products and an exaggerated reliance on market surveys, and a frequent recourse to takeover bids against firms rich in cash reserves and to mergers that minimize competition, diversify operations, and stabilize corporate income.

The exodus of Canadian corporations from Quebec, which seems almost a concerted movement, does not mean that Toronto is assuming the commanding situation which Montreal enjoyed all through the nineteenth century and becoming the economic centre of the country. This is now an impossible role for any one city or region. There is a strong tendency for power to be dispersed across the country, with the west making the most spectacular gains and acquiring matching political influence. Even though Toronto is the most powerful city in Canada, it cannot take on the coordination of the country's industrial and financial activity as English Montreal did in the previous century. The drive, the imagination, and the opportunity are no longer there.

It is frequently stated that the Quebec economy has suffered from the negative effects of nationalist and separatist agitation. What is more likely is that it has suffered from the breakdown of the Ontario-Quebec axis, of which that agitation has been a manifestation. However, the end of the domination exerted by the two central provinces over the rest of the country must have a direct effect on Ontario as well. Indeed, this is what has taken place; the provincial economy has slowed down and unemployment has reached a level which the North American recession alone does not explain. The inability of English-language management to accommodate the French-speaking middle class, together with the Ontario government's refusal to be more generous towards the French population of that province, has contributed in undermining the basis for its prosperity. It has caused Quebec to challenge established relationships. The Canadian political order was further weakened by agitation in the Western provinces for a greater measure of economic independence from the central provinces.

The confusion surrounding the present situation contradicts the premises underlying Pierre Trudeau's concept of federalism and René Lévesque's concept of sovereignty-association. The foundations of the Canadian economy have undergone such divisive transformations that the country's political unity must be now defined in a way that is entirely new. The very absence of a consensus on the nature of the federal system makes it impossible for Quebec to negotiate an effective agreement on any form of political sovereignty and economic association with Canada. In any event, the common market that Premier Lévesque has in mind rests on a vision of the Canadian economy that is now obsolete.

While there is marked uncertainty about economic and political trends in English Canada, French Quebec exhibits a newfound confidence in the future after a fifteen-year period of doubt and anxiety. It seeks to expand the psychological borders which it had imposed on its own activities but which it now finds much too narrow. At the same time it wants to be free of the crushing limitations which collective goals impose on personal expression and ambitions.

However, no one in Quebec seems aware that English Canada is increasingly disposed to question the values associated with liberalism and individualism. There is no apparent concern about the possibility that the Canadian business establishment, and the population of Ontario and other English-speaking provinces, may react negatively to the impact of French expansionism. Having practically abandoned the Quebec market to French-speaking managers and having contributed to the creation of new linguistic boundaries within the country, large Canadian corporations may well be tempted to form a coalition to arrest the political and economic changes set in motion by the new class of French-speaking managers. These are problems which could certainly temper the enthusiasm of those Quebecers who are now rediscovering the exhilarating satisfaction of personal effort and initiative. But this prospect is too remote to attract any attention at the present time.

For the time being, Quebec is completely absorbed in the task of transforming its ideology and its world view. There is an identifiable movement away from the traditional elitism and its attachment to a utopian idealism bound up with the concept of nationhood. There is also a certain desire to overturn the monstrous bureaucratic apparatus which has managed over a period of twenty years to direct the modernization of French society. Similarly, the type of nationalism which helped make French Quebec into a cohesive society is losing its effectiveness as a prime motivating force. The institutions and the attitudes inherited from the past are being reexamined critically.

This movement is inspired by the need for action and by the adoption of a more pragmatic assessment of ideas and situations. There is a pronounced inclination to accept the world as it is, which means that optimism, paradoxically, is slowly coming to overshadow the sense of justice. History with all its contradictions and its disappointments is being accepted without the need to reinterpret it in the light of various nationalist causes. In this more relaxed political climate, culture assumes a personal rather than a collective meaning and its newly discovered relativism works to dampen the confrontations between French- and English-speaking people.

Inevitably, nationalist animosity towards everything English begins to be perceived in a different light. The strange and obsessional character it has assumed since the 1970s appears so excessive that it can be interpreted only as a way of delaying change while mentalities slowly adjust to the impending reversal in expectations. Thus, historical grievances sink back into history. The cultural anxiety incorporated into political programs subsides as a result of the self-confidence which individuals display in their own actions. There is now a new sense of identity, both personal and collective, which amounts to self-acceptance.

Significantly, it is a return to the original meaning of Quebec's official motto, composed in more serene times: *Je me souviens. Je suis né sous le lys et j'ai grandi sous la rose.*

Epilogue

With the reelection of the Parti Québécois on 13 April 1981, nationalism remained the official ideology of the government and it continued to dominate the mental universe of a majority of French-speaking people in Quebec. The margin of victory had been a relatively narrow one. Nevertheless, the general view was that the Parti Québécois had managed to consolidate itself in power and that it would likely stay in office for quite some time without fear of an effective opposition.

Throughout the election campaign, there was an obvious reluctance to abandon the modes of thought which had come to the fore at the time of the Quiet Revolution and which had subsequently become identified with nationalist sentiment. Even for those who entertained gnawing doubts about the current situation, it was difficult to break the habitual dependence on opinion leaders and intellectual elites who were constantly asserting the preeminence of collective goals.

In these circumstances, Claude Ryan's call for individualism and self-reliance was greeted with a certain feeling of apprehension. It proved difficult for a great many voters to translate newly acquired attitudes and expectations into a vote for Claude Ryan and the Liberal party. It was as if French Quebec was not yet ready to make that kind of leap voluntarily and as a matter of deliberate choice. It was a period of ambiguity and indecisiveness.

Curiously enough, the same kind of apprehension had been displayed less than a year earlier at the time of the referendum on the concept of political independence put forward by Premier René Lévesque and the Parti Québécois. In this instance too, the majority had expressed its reluctance to support sweeping changes in social outlook and political organization.

Satisfaction with existing conditions and institutions does not explain the refusal of French society to opt for change in one direction or the other. The signs of discontent are too obvious to support that kind of interpretation. Impatience with the rising costs of the welfare state and the economic burden of government bureaucracy are beginning to shape political thinking. The psychological energy generated by nationalism now seems almost totally spent as a growing number of people manifest their weariness at being constantly regimented in the service of nationalist causes. Similarly, there is a generalized skepticism regarding the relevance of federal institutions except for specific economic problems such as energy.

One characteristic shared by the divergent proposals for sovereignty-association and for the acceptance of liberal values is that their endorsement by a majority would have very little prospect of rallying the minority. In other words, the victory of either of these propositions would have profound divisive effects on Quebec society. It is a situation which inspires anxiety, possibly because of the memory of the October Crisis of 1970 and the application of the War Measures Act which followed. A large number of people are unconditionally opposed to the creation of new barriers between Quebec and the rest of Canada. Similarly, there is a sizable minority that would categorically oppose any government in power inspired by the kind of values propounded by Liberal leader Claude Ryan.

It is as if Quebec feared for the internal cohesion which the Quiet Revolution had restored and consolidated. It shied away instinctively from any collective decision that might compromise its historic ability to withstand the pressures of English-speaking North America and retain its distinctive cultural identity.

Support for federalism and attachment to nationalist values may after all have played a rather negligible role in the contradictory verdicts given by Quebec voters in the referendum and in the ensuing general election. The foremost consideration may well have been the desire to postpone for some time any decision affecting Quebec's basic social structure.

Again, there is a strong element of indecisiveness and ambiguity in such a course. But one must also consider the possibility that the choices being offered by political leaders were not considered appropriate or relevant, that they did not provide for adequate guidelines for the future. This touches on the peculiar relationship between the people and their elites in Quebec.

Throughout its history in Quebec, French society has consistently given the impression of being a docile mass in the hands of its recognized elites and of sometimes being swayed by skilful agitators bent on challenging the established order. Yet on numerous occasions, the supposed passivity of the population has been found to be a myth. The unexpected drop in the birth rate during the 1950s and the abandonment of traditional religious values during the 1960s were realized in the face of deep misgivings on the part of governing elites at the time. The same could be said of the long-term exodus from farm to city as well as of the rise of the Créditiste movement which challenged the preeminence of the educated classes. In each instance the official view was that group values were being undermined.

The independence of mind exhibited by the population and the very great distances sometimes separating it from its elites help to explain why Quebec politics so often moves by fits and starts and in unexpected directions. The electoral defeat of both sovereignty-association and Claude Ryan's new liberalism would therefore suggest that Quebec is once again involved in a periodic mutation that no leadership is capable of directing or containing.

Such events occur when French society seeks to work out a new equilibrium that will balance its own internal drives against the pressures exerted upon it by the rest of North America. The main trends perceptible at the beginning of the 1980s are the rise of individualism and the desire for personal achievement, a greater interest in economic management, and a temporary rejection of the historical collectivism that has allowed the precarious survival of French culture.

Outside pressures have contributed in reinforcing these internal trends. Inflation, coupled with the monetarist policies of the Reagan administration in the United States, has undermined the welfare state and the type of egalitarian social democracy favoured by the intellectual elite and moderate left-wing elements that happen to be in power. The Lévesque government has been forced to cut back on social services and to assume an unyielding stance in preparation for the next round of collective bargaining with public service unions.

These somewhat painful readjustments have been presented as the results of straightforward policy decisions devoid of ideological connotations. The government is not inclined to view current problems in the light of far-reaching changes in mentalities which would inevitably bring about sweeping transformations in social organization and economic activity. On the contrary, it views budget constraints as temporary setbacks on the road to social justice and political independence. It is all the more inclined to be optimistic about the achievement of nationalist goals now that the Liberal opposition in the National Assembly has been demoralized by its electoral defeat and is hardly offering any valid criticism of government policies.

From all appearances, nationalism remains strong and it survives as the dominant ideology in Quebec. However, as the gap between personal expectations and public attitudes becomes wider, its character becomes increasingly rhetorical and it is no longer able to give voice to the original dynamic impulses that made it into such a potent political force.

Since the reelection of the Parti Québécois, nationalism is no longer an instrument of collective mobilization. It is now in the service of conformity and even of repression. It will continue as a framework for political thinking until a clear ideological alternative asserts itself and until the population has become conscious of the need for change. But its decline has already started.

Suggestions for Further Reading

Arnopoulos, Sheila McLeod, and Clift, Dominique. *The English Fact in Quebec.* Montreal: McGill-Queen's University Press, 1980.

Bélanger, André. *L'apolitisme des idéologies québécoises: le grand tournant, 1934–1936.* Québec: Les Presses de l'Université Laval, 1974.

Benjamin, Jacques. *Planification et politique au Québec.* Montréal: Les Presses de l'Université de Montréal, 1974.

Bergeron, Gérard. *Le Canada-Français après deux siècles de patience.* Paris: Editions du Seuil, 1967.

———. *L'indépendance, oui mais....* Montréal: Editions Quinze, 1977.

Bergeron, Léandre. *The History of Quebec: A Patriote's Handbook.* Toronto: NC Press, 1975.

Bourgault, Pierre. *Oui à l'indépendance du Québec.* Montréal: Editions Quinze, 1977.

Brunet, Michel. *Canadians et Canadiens.* Montréal: Fides, 1954.

———. *Québec-Canada Anglais: deux itinéraires, un affrontement.* Montréal: Editions HMH, 1968.

Cameron, David. *Nationalism, Self-determination and the Quebec Question.* Toronto: Macmillan of Canada, 1974.

Cook, Ramsay. *Canada and the French-Canadian Question.* Toronto: Macmillan of Canada, 1966.

———. *The Maple Leaf Forever: Essays on Nationalism and Politics in Canada.* 2nd ed. Toronto: Macmillan of Canada, 1977.

———, ed. *French-Canadian Nationalism: An Anthology.* Toronto: Macmillan of Canada, 1969.

Desbarats, Peter. *René: A Canadian in Search of a Country.* Toronto: McClelland and Stewart, 1976.

Dion, Léon. *Quebec, the Unfinished Revolution.* Montréal: McGill-Queen's University Press, 1976.

——— *Nationalismes et politique au Québec.* Montréal: Hurtubise HMH, 1975.

Dumont, Fernand. *The Vigil of Quebec.* Toronto: University of Toronto Press, 1974.

Grand'maison, Jacques. *La nouvelle classe et l'avenir du Québec.* Montréal: Stanké, 1979.

Groulx, Lionel. *Abbé Groulx: Variations on a Nationalist Theme.* Edited by Susan Mann Trofimenkoff. Toronto: Copp Clark Pub., 1973.

Guindon, Hubert. "Social Unrest, Social Class and Quebec's Bureaucratic Revolution." *Queen's Quarterly*, Summer 1964, pp. 150–62.

Jacobs, Jane. *The Question of Separatism: Quebec and the Struggle Over Sovereignty.* New York: Random House, 1980.

Johnson, Daniel. *Egalité ou indépendance.* Montréal: Editions Renaissance, 1965.

Jones, Richard. *Community in Crisis: French-Canadian Nationalism in Perspective.* Toronto: McClelland and Stewart, 1967.

Joy, Richard J. *Languages in Conflict: The Canadian Experience.* Toronto: McClelland and Stewart, 1972.

Laurendeau, André. *Witness for Quebec.* Edited and translated by Philip Stratford. Toronto: Macmillan of Canada, 1973.

Laurendeau, Marc. *Les Québécois violents.* Montréal: Boréal Express, 1974.

Lévesque, René. *An Option for Quebec.* Toronto: McClelland and Stewart, 1968.

McWhinney, Edward. *Quebec and the Constitution, 1960–1978.* Toronto: University of Toronto Press, 1979.

Milner, S. H., and Milner, H. *The Decolonization of Quebec: An Analysis of Left-Wing Nationalism.* Toronto: McClelland and Stewart, 1973.

Monière, Denis. *Ideologies in Quebec: The Historical Development.* Toronto: University of Toronto Press, 1981.

Morin, Michel, and Bertrand, Claude. *Le territoire imaginaire de la culture.* Montréal: Hurtubise HMH, 1979.

Murray, Vera. *Le Parti québécois: de la fondation à la prise du pouvoir.* Montréal: Hurtubise HMH, 1976.

Ouellet, Fernand. *Lower Canada, Social Change and Nationalism, 1791–1840.* Toronto: McClelland and Stewart, 1980.

Reid, Malcolm. *The Shouting Signpainters: A Literary and Political Account of Quebec Revolutionary Nationalism.* Toronto: McClelland and Stewart, 1972.

Rioux, Marcel. *Quebec in Question.* Toronto: J. Lewis and Samuel, 1971.

Roy, Jean-Louis. *La marche des Québécois: le temps des ruptures.* Montréal: Leméac, 1976.

Ryerson, Stanley. *Unequal Union: Roots of Crisis in the Canadas, 1815–1873.* Toronto: Progress Books, 1973.

Smiley, David V. *Canada in Question: Federalism in the Seventies.* 2nd ed. Toronto: McGraw-Hill Ryerson, 1975.

Trofimenkoff, Susan Mann. *Action Française: French Canadian Nationalism in the Twenties.* Toronto: University of Toronto Press, 1975.

Trudeau, Pierre Elliott. *Federalism and the French Canadians.* Toronto: Macmillan of Canada, 1968.